Guy & MARILYN EMERY
UPTON, NEW YORK
JUNE 27, 1965

# THE SWISS AND THEIR MOUNTAINS

*also by Sir Arnold Lunn*

A CENTURY OF MOUNTAINEERING

1 CASPAR WOLF (1735–1783). Schiltwald river and view of the Lauterbrunnen valley, perhaps the earliest winter picture of the Alps. Gouache. (Graphic collection of the Federal Polytechnical School in Zurich)

# THE SWISS
# AND
# THEIR MOUNTAINS

A STUDY OF THE INFLUENCE OF
MOUNTAINS ON MAN

BY

SIR ARNOLD LUNN

*London*
GEORGE ALLEN & UNWIN LTD
RUSKIN HOUSE MUSEUM STREET

PRINTED IN GREAT BRITAIN
*in 11 point Juliana type*
BY SIMSON SHAND LTD
LONDON, HERTFORD AND HARLOW

TO KARL WEBER

# PREFACE

The Swiss Alpine Club will celebrate its centenary in 1963, and I hope that they will accept this book as a token of gratitude on behalf of all mountaineers who have enjoyed the hospitality of the huts which they have built throughout the Swiss Alps, and who have read with interest and profit the publications of the Club.

*The Swiss and their Mountains* is not, however, intended to be a history of the Swiss Alpine Club or of Swiss mountaineering. It is rather, as is stated on the title page, a study of the influence of mountains on man. There are, of course, chapters on the achievements of Swiss mountaineers from the days of the pioneers to modern times but, as is clear from the list of contents, there are many other aspects of the relations between the Swiss and their mountains which will be discussed in this book, as, for instance, the contribution of the Swiss to mountain art. Thanks to the generosity of the Swiss Foundation for Alpine Research, which commissioned the book and met the expense of the blocks, it has been possible to include in this book a representative collection of reproductions in colour of the mountain artists of Switzerland.

ARNOLD LUNN

## ACKNOWLEDGMENTS

*The publication of this book in its present form has been made possible through the co-operation and generous support of the Swiss Foundation for Alpine Research.*

# CONTENTS

# ILLUSTRATIONS

# I

## THE MOUNTAIN MATRIX

SWITZERLAND is today an independent country not because her mountains are a barrier to the invader, for no mountains separate Geneva from France or Basle from Germany, but because a passion for independence seems a natural growth in mountain valleys, and because it has always been far easier for emperors and other rulers to assert their authority over the dwellers in the lowlands than over the natives of remote mountain valleys. It was therefore no accident that the revolt which laid the foundation of what we now know as Switzerland should have begun on the shores of a lake ringed round with rugged peaks.

The role of the mountains in the creation of an independent country was not restricted to that spirit of independence which the mountains foster, but also, as we shall see, to the historic accident that the men of Uri controlled the pass of the St Gotthard, and to the fact that the decisive battle of Morgarten was fought in a mountain pass by mountain men.

The Lake of the Four Forest Cantons (Vierwaldstättersee), known to the English as Lake Lucerne, derives its name from the Cantons of Uri, Schwyz, Unterwalden and Lucerne, the first three being the founders of the Swiss Confederation, and the Canton of Lucerne being the first Canton to join the young Confederation after their successful revolt against the Habsburgs.

The relations between the Holy Roman Empire and the founders of the Swiss Confederation were, as we shall see, of decisive importance. The Empire was something more than a mere system of government. It was 'a fashion of conceiving the world', an assertion of the fact that the unity of Christendom was not only spiritual but political. The Pope was the spiritual, the Emperor the political head of Christendom. *Una chiesa in uno stato*. The German king only became Holy Roman Emperor

13

after his coronation by the Pope. It was only after the reign of Maximilian I of Austria that the Imperial Crown became hereditary and was assumed by the Emperor of Austria on his succession. When Rudolf of Habsburg, who took his name from a castle the ruins of which can be reached in an hour from Lucerne, was elected German king in 1273, the crown was not hereditary but elective, and the chief object of the electors was to prevent the German king and Holy Roman Emperor from acquiring real power. Rudolf of Habsburg was not an obscure member of the minor nobility of Aarau, as historians once believed, for even at that time the Habsburgs were already in possession of great estates in Alsace, but the electors probably felt that they would be better able to safeguard their interests if they elected a Swiss noble rather than a powerful German prince.

As German king, Rudolf of Habsburg was able to invest his son Albrecht with the Duchy of Austria, and thereafter the Habsburgs became identified with Austria. Rudolf's son, Albrecht, was elected German king in 1298, and was murdered in 1308 by his nephew, Johannes, Duke of Austria. From 1308 to 1438 no Habsburg again wore the Imperial Crown, a fact which is of decisive importance in the history of Switzerland, for it was by exploiting the rivalry between the Habsburgs and the Emperor that the men of Uri and Schwyz and Unterwalden were able to lay the foundations of their independence.

The first object of the Forest Cantons was to secure *Reichsunmittelbarkeit*, that is to say, to place themselves under the immediate lordship of the Emperor. They preferred the rule of the Emperor to the rule of the Habsburgs for many reasons, of which the most important was that they preferred the remote control of the Emperor to the control of the Habsburgs on the doorstep. The Emperor was a long way off, and far less efficient as a tax collector than the Habsburgs. To be directly subject to the Emperor was a status as near to actual independence as the Forest Cantons could ever hope to achieve.

The Emperor was all the readier to support the Forest Cantons because the men of Uri, who were under the immediate lordship of the Emperor, controlled the northern entrance to the Gotthard Pass. The St Gotthard was not 'opened' in the twelfth century, as every Swiss history that I have read implies. The pass was known in Roman times. But some time between 1180 and 1190 the St Gotthard route was *shortened* by rendering the passage of the Schöllenen Gorge practicable, and from that moment the St Gotthard replaced the Lukmanier as the best route from Germany into Italy. The new importance of the St Gotthard was reflected in the status of the Forest Cantons. The Habsburgs were determined to control the approach to the St Gotthard; the Hohenstaufen emperors were equally convinced that the relative independence of the Forest Cantons was of primary importance to them, since they could not afford to allow the Habsburgs to cut them off from the main approach to Italy. The Forest Cantons, as we shall see, won their independence by playing off the Habsburgs against the Emperor. Even when a Habsburg was himself Emperor, the Forest Cantons never allowed the Habsburgs to confuse the rights which they enjoyed *qua* Emperor with the rights which they enjoyed *qua* Habsburg.

It is impossible to exaggerate the importance of the St Gotthard in the struggle for independence. The increasing traffic across this pass transformed many of the men of Uri from agriculturalists into traders. Many of them made a living by providing mules or acting as guides across the pass. Moreover, the traffic across the pass exposed the Forest Cantons to the new wind of freedom which was blowing from Italy, where the communes were fighting an unsuccessful war of liberation against the Emperor. The legend, according to which the men of the Forest Cantons had preserved their passion for liberty thanks to their remoteness from the great world, is the exact reverse of the truth. On the contrary, as the Swiss historian William Martin points out, it was at the moment that this remoteness ceased that the movement for independence began.

This book is not a history of Switzerland but a study of the Swiss in relation to their mountains, and I am therefore only concerned with the struggle for independence, which I have described as greater length in my book, *The Cradle of Switzerland*, because of the decisive influence of the mountains in general and of the two mountain passes in particular, the St Gotthard and Morgarten, on the events which led to the foundation of the Confederation.

The Tell legend, which would seem to have some basis in fact, bears witness to that growing spirit of independence which finally determined the Habsburgs to organize a punitive expedition against the men of the Forest Cantons. For a quarter of a century these mountain men had befriended all their enemies, had not concealed their enthusiastic support and approval of the assassins of Albrecht, and the time had come to teach them a lesson.

Meanwhile, the Forest Cantons were not passively awaiting the Habsburg onslaught. They numbered among their warriors many who had served for years in foreign wars, particularly under the Hohenstaufen. There is no basis whatsoever for the legend which represents them as simple mountain peasants, untutored in the art of war. Their preparations had begun as early as 1290, and by the time the punitive expedition left Zug, the land approach through Arth was already sealed off by a fence of palisades which stretched from the Rigi to the Rüfiberg. A second line of defence had been constructed near the Enge of Oberarth. The Renggpass and the Brünig had also been fortified. The Habsburgs enjoyed a virtual command of the lake, but the ports of Brunnen and Buochs were fortified, and the Forest Cantons did not confine themselves to passive defence. By a series of spirited sorties on the lake against the Habsburg ports, they maintained an active war of nerves.

In the autumn of 1315, Duke Leopold of Austria mobilized his army in Aargau. 'The men of his army,' writes a contemporary chronicler, Joannes Vitoduranus, 'came together with one purpose—utterly to subdue and humiliate those peasants who were surrounded with mountains as with walls.'

On November 15, 1315, the Duke and his knights approached the pass of Morgarten which the men of the Forest Cantons had deliberately left undefended, hoping to lure the Habsburgs into a trap.

They climbed slowly, in single file, towards the pass, their line of battle necessarily broken. Near the top of the pass the leaders halted and looked anxiously up towards the steep hillsides, down which a few stray rocks and pebbles had just fallen. Suddenly an avalanche of huge boulders and tree-trunks crashed down the slopes. The narrow pass of Morgarten was turned into a death-trap—a desperate struggling confusion of men and horses. And then came the human avalanche, an irresistible torrent of peasants swinging their deadly halberds. Beneath these rude weapons the chivalry of the Empire fell. Some died on the

LA LUTSCHINEN SORTANT DU GLACIER INFÉRIEUR DU GRINDELWALD.

Canton de Berne, Province d'Interlaken.

*Dediée à Son Excellence Monsieur de Kalitcheff,*
*Chambellan actuel et Envoyé extraordinaire et M.re Plénipotentiaire de Sa M.té Impératrice de toutes les Russies*
*auprès de LL. HH. Puissances les EE. G. des Provinces-unies.*

*Très ... très humble et très obéissant serviteur J.R. Beälzi.*

2  CASPAR WOLF (1735–1783). Lower Grindelwald glacier. Coloured copper engraving. (From: «Merkwürdige Prospekte aus den Schweizergebirgen», Bern 1776)

spot, others were driven into the lake, while others were killed by falling boulders. Morgarten was perhaps the first battle of the Middle Ages in which an army of mounted knights was beaten by peasants on foot.

On December 9, 1315, the Confederates renewed their first league at the village of Brunnen, and three years later the Dukes of Austria decided to make peace with them.

The Confederation rapidly expanded. Lucerne was naturally the first to join. Zürich, Glarus, Zug and Berne all followed the example of Lucerne in the course of the following year. The growth in strength of the young Confederation was, of course, viewed with alarm by Austria.

The Habsburgs made two attempts to revenge Morgarten, only to suffer crushing defeats at Sempach, ten miles from Lucerne, in 1386, and Näfels in the Canton of Glarus in 1388. After various attempts to seduce Zürich from the Confederation, Austria accepted the inevitable, and signed a treaty of peace. From this time forward the young Confederation, though still within the Empire, was no longer of it. The Germans began to speak of the citizens of this Confederation as *Schweizer*, after Schwyz. The battles of Morgarten, Sempach and Näfels planted the seeds of modern Switzerland. The Cantons which resisted the Habsburgs began as a league of small states within the Empire and emerged a nation. Their success was the more surprising because at that very time the liberties so gallantly defended on the shores of the Lake of Lucerne were being trampled underfoot in Germany. In Germany the monarchial principle was in the ascendant, and the Leagues of the Swabian cities and of the Rhine cities were being crushed. In Switzerland, on the other hand, the principles of a primitive democracy were established on an enduring foundation. Why this contrast? Surely because the primitive Swiss democracy was a natural development in mountain valleys too remote from centres of government to be effectively controlled. The structure of the mountains in which communications between valley and valley are seldom easy is favourable to the development of self-government in the mountain communities. Life in these mountain valleys was never easy, an unending battle against Nature which compelled the mountain dwellers to co-operate closely in the building of paths, in irrigation and in the construction of

B

barriers to avalanches. It was indeed this inevitable co-operation which created a whole range of communal rights, such as grazing rights on the cattle alps.

In the charter of August 1, 1291, which established the young Confederation, there is no challenge to the rights of the distant Emperor. The Confederates were content to remain members of the Holy Roman Empire but there is a firm repudiation of the rule of the Habsburg Landvogts and a stubborn insistence on the rights of the Confederates to appoint all those responsible for the government of their communities, judges for instance.

In England democracy was something which was gradually conceded from above, in Switzerland democracy evolved from below. It is only in my own lifetime the word 'democracy' has lost its pejorative sense in England. My father was an ardent Liberal but he never talked about democracy. Eighteenth-century Whigs and nineteenth-century Liberals distrusted democracy. Archdeacon Coxe travelling through eighteenth-century Switzerland noted with *surprise* that many of the Canton were well governed, 'not withstanding the natural defects of a democratic constitution', and as late as 1866 Gladstone in proposing an extension of the franchise repudiated indignantly the accusation that he was advocating democracy. 'You will exclaim,' he said, 'that this is democracy. I reply it is no such thing.' Switzerland, on the other hand, was built not on feudal but on democratic foundations and bears the clear imprint of the mountain matrix.

# 2

## THE PIONEERS

'A HIGHLY intelligent Swiss guide,' writes Leslie Stephen, 'once gazed with me upon the dreary expanse of chimney-pots through which the South-Western Railway escapes from this dingy metropolis. Fancying that I rightly interpreted his looks as symptomatic of the proverbial homesickness of mountaineers, I remarked with an appropriate sigh, "That is not so fine a view as we have seen together from the top of Mont Blanc." "Ah, sir!" was his pathetic reply, "it is far finer!" '

If not finer, at least more exciting to a guide who has never seen a big city.

Was Stephen's 'highly intelligent guide' a typical Bergler[1] in his reaction to mountain scenery? The typical Bergler does not write books. Indeed, many of them can only with difficulty be persuaded to answer urgent letters. It would therefore be rash to base any final conclusions on the fact that the first articulate lovers of the mountains were professors in Zürich and Berne. Again, it is no accident that there is no poetry and no romance in the names which Berglers gave to their native mountains. There are innumerable white mountains (Mont Blanc, Weisshorn, Dent Blanche), black mountains (Schwarzhorn, Aiguille Noire de Peuteret), green mountains (Aiguille Verte, Grünhorn), and many peaks which served as primitive sundials for indicating midday (Mittaghorn, Dent du Midi, Aiguille du Midi), but I cannot think of a beautiful mountain name which

[1] Bergler. No translation of this word, derived from Berg (mountain), such as 'mountain men', seems to be adequate to convey the characteristics of the Berglers with whom I have climbed and skied. When Colonel Roger Bonvin was elected a Bundesrat, the Neue Zürcher Zeitung (Sept. 27, '62) reminded its readers that Colonel Bonvin was president of the Swiss Ski Association and wrote, 'Mit dem kleinen zähen Walliser Roger Bonvin ist der Typ des schweizerischen Bergler in den Bundesrat eingezogen.' ('With the small sturdy Walliser Roger Bonvin the type of the Swiss Berglers is represented in the Bundesrat.')

was not invented by modern mountaineers or, in rare cases, by those Berglers whose horizons had been widened in their training for the priesthood. Thus Adlerpass, Col des Hirondelles, Aiguilles Dorées, Wellenkuppe and Dent du Requin were all so named by English mountaineers, the Dom (cathedral) by the priest of Randa, and the Jungfrau by the Augustinian monks of Interlaken because the radiant white curves of the Jungfrau reminded them of the Augustinian nuns who were clothed in white and who had a house in Interlaken.

It was not until the beginning of the sixteenth century that there is any *literary* evidence of Swiss deriving enjoyment either from mountain scenery or from mountain walks. 'It is known,' writes Francis Gribble in his scholarly book, *The Early Mountaineers*, 'that there were ascents of Pilatus as early as 1518, and there is reason to believe that the excursion was not even then regarded as a novelty.'

*Johann Müller*

The first description by a Swiss of the ascent of a mountain for pleasure is a poem in rather indifferent Latin hexameters, the *Stockhorniad*, which describes the ascent in 1536 of a minor peak above Thun, the Stockhorn (7,912 feet above the sea). The author was a professor of Berne University, Johann Müller, and the poem is dedicated to one of his companions on the expedition, Dr Peter Cunzen, a botanist.

The party started from Erlenbach in the Simmenthal, and the account of the climb and of the descent includes an elaborate description of the two excellent meals consumed on the climb, the meal on the top and the two meals on the descent. Some forty-five lines are devoted to feeding, whereas the summit panorama is worth only five lines:

> unde sub ortum
> Stagna, lacus, torrentes Simmae, Arulae que fluenta,
> Oppida spectamus campos, viridantia prata.
> Occiduas sed equos ubi Phoebus mergit in undas
> Innumeros montes speculamur, ut acquora lata.

which Mr Gribble translates:

> Whence, looking down
> Eastward we see lakes, marshes and a town,

The torrents of the Simmenthal—to West
Mountains like billows on the sea's broad breast.

Mr Gribble's translation, though rather livelier than the original, recaptures the jovial gusto of the *Stockhorniad* and, as nothing in the poem suggests that Müller felt that the expedition was in any way reasonable or unusual, it is a fair deduction that by the beginning of the sixteenth century the ascent of easily accessible mountain tops was of not infrequent occurence. It was, indeed, on the summit of the Stockhorn that Professor Marti of Berne, a sixteenth-century mountain lover, discovered a Greek inscription cut in to a stone,

ὀτῶν ὀρῶν ἔρως ἄριστος

which may be rendered 'the love of mountains is best'.

### Early Ascents of Pilatus

Pilatus (6,965 feet), above Lucerne, was the first Alpine peak to emerge from obscurity when mountains first ceased to be regarded with a mixture of abhorrence and indifference. It was not to the view of the mountain from Lucerne or to the panorama from its summit that Pilatus owed this distinction, but to the legendary association of the mountain with Pontius Pilate, legendary because the mountain probably owes its name not to Pontius Pilate but to the Latin word *pileatus* (capped), Pilatus often being capped with cloud.

Conrad Gesner, in his *Descriptio Montis Fracti Juxta Lucernam*, quotes the history of the legend from the works of the thirteenth-century writer Jacobus Voragine, Bishop of Genoa. Pontius Pilate, according to this story, was condemned by the Emperor Tiberius, who decreed that he should be put to death in the most shameful possible manner. Hearing this, Pilate promptly committed suicide. Tiberius concealed his chagrin, and philosophically remarked that a man whose own hand had not spared him, had most certainly died the most shameful of deaths. Pilate's body was attached to a stone and flung into the Tiber, where it caused a succession of terrible storms. The Romans therefore took the body out of the Tiber and finally deposited it in the Rhône. 'But there too,' writes the Bishop, 'the evil spirits were present, carrying out the same operations as before. Consequently the inhabitants, unable to edure this molestation of the Devils, got rid of the phial from which curses overflowed upon them, and sent the body to be buried in the territory of Lausanne. But the people of Lausanne, finding themselves distressed by the troubles which they had been told would overtake them, moved it on again, and dropped it into a well surrounded by mountains, where, according to some accounts, certain diabolic machinations and ebullitions are still seen.'

The marsh in question, Gesner adds, is the little marshy lake near the summit of Pilatus. Pilate gave less trouble on Pilatus than elsewhere, but he disapproved of people who threw stones into the lake, and avenged himself by stirring up tempests. Once a year he escaped from the waters, and sat clothed in a scarlet robe on a rock near by. Anybody luckless enough to see him on these occasions died within the twelve-month.

So much for the story, which was firmly believed by the citizens of Lucerne. Access to the lake was forbidden, unless the visitor was accompanied by a respectable burgher, pledged to veto any practices that Pilate might consider a slight. In 1307, six clergymen were imprisoned for having attempted an ascent without observing the local regulations. It is even said that climbers were occasionally put to death for breaking these stringent by-laws. None the less, ascents occasionally took place.

It appears that the mountain was climbed before the beginning of the fourteenth century, and it is probable that Pilatus was twice climbed in 1518, according to tradition by the exiled Duke of Württemberg, and without doubt by four Swiss scholars, Joachim von Watt, who wrote under the name of Vadianus, Zimmerman and Genshäussler of Lucerne, and Grebel of Zürich.

Joachim von Watt at one time held a professorial chair in Vienna, and later practised for many years in his native place, St Gallen, of which he became burgermeister. His account of the ascent of Pilatus was mainly written to support the belief in the Pilate legend, and particularly of the stirring up of tempests. It was not until 1585, nearly seventy years after von Watt's ascent, that the Pilate legend ceased to command respect. In that year Johann Müller, the Stadtpfarrer of Lucerne, invited as many citizens as cared to join him in an experiment designed to test the truth of the legend. Together they climbed to Pilate's lake, on reaching which the priest flung stone after stone into the lake and shouted contemptuously, '*Pilat wirf aus dein Kath.*' All those present could bear witness that the lake's surface was disturbed by nothing but the ripples where the stones had fallen. Pilate's lamentable failure to react to this gross challenge settled the matter, and the legend which men had been imprisoned for doubting only survived as a picturesque myth with no power to evoke belief.

## Conrad Gesner (1516-1565)

Conrad Gesner, a doctor and professor in Zürich, was the first man whom we know to have made a regular practice of climbing mountains for no other reason than that he derived supreme pleasure from mountain walks. Till then, most of those who found their way to a mountain summit were quite content not to repeat the experiment. A particular ascent was made for a particular purpose, such as scientific curiosity, but, this purpose achieved, the experiment was not repeated.

Gesner, on the other hand, was the protoype of all those who climb because they are happier on a mountain side than in the plains. His own mountain credo was expressed in a letter written in 1543 when Gesner was twenty-seven years of age, to a friend, Vogel von Glarus, whose name was latinized as Avienus:

'Most learned Avienus—I have resolved for the future, so long as God suffers me to live, to climb mountains, or at all events to climb one mountain every year, at the season when vegetation is at its best, partly for the sake of studying botany, and partly for the delight of the mind and the proper exercise of the body. For what, think you, is the pleasure, what the joy of a mind, affected as it should be to marvel at the spectacle of the mighty masses of the mountains, and lift up one's head, as it were, among the clouds. The mind is strangely excited by the amazing altitude, and carried away to the contemplation of the great Architect of the Universe. . . . Cultivators of philosophy will proceed to contemplate the great spectacles of this earthly paradise; and by no means the least of these are steep and broken mountain-tops, the unscaleable precipices, the vast slopes stretching towards the sky, the dark and shady forests.'

Gesner's mountaineering was confined to the lower heights which are relegated by modern mountaineers to the category of training walks, but in those days an ascent of Pilatus was still a great adventure. Certainly Gesner's love for mountains was profounder than that of some modern experts in acrobatic rock climbing. Petrarch was his only predecessor in the literary expression of the mountain cult, and Petrarch, so far as we know, only climbed one mountain, Mont Ventoux.

We have no detailed record of Gesner's climbs, but luckily his account of an ascent of Pilatus still survives, a most sincere tribute to the simple pleasures of the heights. His writing is subjective, and records the impress of simple emotions on an unsophisticated mind. He finds a naive joy in all the elemental things that make up a mountain walk, the cool breezes playing on heated limbs, the sun's genial warmth, the contrasts of outline, colour and height, the unending variety, so that 'in one day you wander through the four seasons of the year, Spring, Summer, Autumn and Winter'. He explains that every sense is delighted, the sense of hearing is gratified by the witty conversation of friends, 'by the songs of the birds, and even by the stillness of the waste'. He adds, on a very modern note, that the mountaineer is freed from the noisy tumult of the city, and that in the 'profound abiding silence one catches echoes of the harmony of celestial spheres'. He anticipates the most enduring reward of the mountaineer, and his words might serve as the motto for a mountain book of today: *'Jucundum erit postea meminisse laborum atque periculorum, juvabit haec animo revolvere et narrare amicis.'* Toil and danger are sweet to recall, every mountaineer loves 'to revolve these in his mind and to tell them to his friends'. Moreover, contrast is the essence of our enjoyment and 'the very delight of rest is intensified when it follows hard labour'. And then Gesner turns with a burst of scorn to his imaginary opponent. 'But, say you, we lack feather beds and mattresses and pillows. Oh, frail and effeminate man! Hay shall take the place of these luxuries. It is soft, it is fragrant. It is blended from healthy grass and flower, and as you sleep respiration will be sweeter and healthier than ever. Your pillow shall be of hay. Your mattress shall be of hay. A blanket of hay shall be thrown across your body.' That is the kind of thing an enthusiastic mountaineer might have written about the club huts in the old days before the hay gave place to mattresses.

There follows an eloquent description of the ascent and an

analysis of the Pilate legend. Thirty years were to pass before Pastor Müller finally disposed of the myth, but Gesner is clearly sceptical, and concludes with the robust assertion that, even if evil spirits exist, they are 'impotent to harm the faithful who worship the one heavenly light, and Christ the Sun of Justice'. A bold challenge to the superstitions of the age, a challenge worthy of the man.

The conventions of the day restricted the professor to the study or to the pulpit, but Gesner, as Mr Gribble rightly remarks, was 'the spiritual ancestor of Agassiz, de Saussure and Tyndall, mountain explorers who were also men of the study and who could have made their own Gesner's tribute to the intellectual rewards of mountaineering.

'I would wish for a man who is moderately robust in mind and body and who has enjoyed a liberal education and is not too given over to laziness, luxury or lust, that he should become a student and an admirer of Nature, and reflect with reverence on the great works of the supreme architect and on the immense variety of natural beauty revealed among the mountains, often indeed to be seen from the slopes of a single eminence, and thus enjoy not only a harmony of the great pleasures of the senses but also of the delights of the intellect.'

### Professor Benedikt Marti of Berne

In his love for the mountains Gesner was ahead of his time, but he had at least one friend who shared his enthusiasm, Professor Marti of Berne.

Marti was the first to pay a tribute to the loveliest of mountain views, the panorama from the terrace of Berne. 'These are the mountains,' he writes, 'which form our pleasure and delight when we gaze at them from the highest parts of our city, and admire their mighty peaks and broken crags that threaten to fall at any moment. Who, then, would not admire, love and willingly visit, explore and climb places of this sort? I should assuredly call those who are not attracted by them dolts, stupid dull fishes, and slow tortoises. I am never happier than on the mountain crests, and there are no wanderings dearer to me than those on the mountains' (written in 1557).

This passage suggests that an appreciation of mountain

scenery was less exceptional in the sixteenth century than the scanty evidence for such appreciation in literature might suggest. For if there had been a virtual concensus of opinion among educated people that mountains were repulsive, Marti would surely have adopted a more defensive attitude, and at least given his reasons for finding pleasure, not only in the beauty of the mountains as seen from below but also for his delight in the attempt 'to explore and climb places of this sport'. Instead, he assumes that every right-minded man shares his tastes, and that those who do not may reasonably be compared with 'stupid dull fishes and slow tortoises'.

*Josias Simler (1530-1576)*
Long before men began to climb peaks for fun, travellers crossed mountain passes because the pass was the shortest route to their destination. Even glacier passes have been crossed from time immemorial. Roman coins, for instance, have been discovered on the summit of the Théodule pass which connects Zermatt in Switzerland with Breuil in Italy.

Josias Simler, a clergyman and professor at Zürich, was the first to write a textbook of mountain craft. His book, *De Alpibus Commentarius*, published in 1574, provides evidence of the comparative frequency with which glacier passes were traversed in the earliest times. Simler is familiar with the use not only of alpenstocks *(hos alpinos baculos vocant)* but also crampons which only came into general use among modern mountaineers at the end of the nineteenth century. 'To counteract the slipperiness of the ice they attach shoes, like horseshoes, to their feet, with three sharp spikes on them *(tribus acutis cuspidibus praeditas)*.'

All that he has to say about the use of the rope on snow-covered glaciers as a protection against concealed crevasses, of spectacles as a protection against snow-blindness, and of paper as a protection against cold, is sensible and needs no revision today. Of Alpine guides he writes, 'These men tie ropes round their waists, to which the travellers are also tied, and the leader tests the snow with a long pole, and scrutinizes it with care in the search for crevasses. If, however, a careless man falls into a crevasse, he is held by the rope, and pulled out by his friends who are on the same rope.'

He describes in some detail the nature of avalanches, and is aware that a man can live for some time under an avalanche. 'If he can move his hands about and clear a little space round him before the snow hardens, he can breathe under the snow and may even live for two or three days.'

There is, however, not one line in his work which hints at any liking for the mountains. He was writing for travellers who were *forced* to cross mountain passes, and who had no more affection for the mountains than a seasick traveller for the Straits of Dover. On the contrary, he seems to be writing for those who shared his own horror of narrow paths winding up precipices. (*Plerumque ante prospectus ex his locis in profundissimas valles subjectas, magnum horrorem transeuntibus incutit.*)

Whereas Gesner's personality emerges in his writings, we know almost as little about Simler himself at the end as at the beginning of his book. Gesner is concerned not only with the mountains as objective facts but also with his own highly personal reactions to mountain beauty. Simler, on the other hand, can only see in the mountains inconvenient barriers which travellers in general and merchants in particular have to cross. As a practical man he did his best to clarify what was known about snowcraft and icecraft, an old science even in his day.

If we could charter H. G. Wells's Time Machine and join Gesner on a mountain path we should enjoy a gossip about mountains and why we feel about them as we do, and our respective preferences for particular mountain views, and we should part from him with affectionate regret. But if the same Time Machine transported us to Simler's study in Zürich, we should be assured of a welcome if we brought with us Mr Gerald Seligman's scientific study of snow and avalanche craft, but that wonderful chapter in Leslie Stephen's classic on 'The Regrets of a Mountaineer' would mean nothing to him. The only regrets which he could understand would be those of a mountain traveller who was forced to cross the mountains on his way to and from Italy.

Gesner is one of us, a founding father of the society of mountain lovers; Simler, the first to attempt a systematic analysis of mountain craft, might be described as the father of mountain scientists. He commands our respect, whereas Gesner evokes our affection, but both Gesner and Simler are men of whom Swiss mountaineers have every reason to be proud.

*Johann Jacob Scheuchzer (1672-1733)*
Scheuchzer, like Gesner, was a doctor and professor in Zürich. His reputation as a scientist attracted such attention that on the suggestion of Leibnitz he was invited to take up an appointment at St Petersburg, but he stayed at Zürich and occupied in succcession the chair of mathematics and the chair of physics. Between 1702 and 1711 he spent many university vacations travelling in the mountains, and he describes his experiences in a book with the cumbrous title of οὐρεσιφόιτης *helveticus sive Itinera per Helvetiae Alpinas regiones facta annus 1702-3-4-5-6-7-9-10-11*. The book, in two volumes, is dedicated to the Royal Society, and various Fellows of the Society, including Sir Isaac Newton, contributed to the expenses of publication.

Scheuchzer has much in common both with Gesner and with Simler. His personality emerges, as does Gesner's, from his pages, but like Simler he has no affection for the mountains. Simler's interest began and ended with the practical problems which the mountains presented to the traveller who crossed their passes. Scheuchzer never pretended to enjoy his mountain walks, and constantly complains of the toil which hill walking involves. Characteristically, if inaccurately, he derives the name of Gemmi from the Latin *gemitus,* a groan, because it cannot be climbed without great groans *(quod non nisi cum crebis gemitibus superetur),* and he admits that he did not quite complete the ascent of Pilatus because of 'bodily weariness and the distance still to be traversed'. His final summary of mountain walking is that 'the climbing of mountains takes one's breath away, but may be rendered less disagreeable by pleasant conversation'.

The motive of his mountain expeditions was the pursuit of knowledge. He set the fashion, followed by so many of our own Alpine pioneers, of taking barometrical observations, most of which were hopelessly wrong. But at least he did what he could to make his mountain wanderings serve the cause of science, and he had undoubtedly the makings of a scientist. He held, as we have seen, the chair of physics at Zürich. He achieved distinction as a botanist, and invented a theory to account for the glacier motion which was at least the result of first-hand observation of the facts. He helped to popularize Newton's theories, and published the first map of Switzerland with any claims to accuracy. He was sufficiently in advance of his age to campaign for the abolition of the death penalty for witches.

Scheuchzer reminds me of Sir Thomas Browne, for like Browne he had a genuinely scientific curiosity, and found it difficult to reject picturesque myths, and when forced to reject them, does so with obvious reluctance. 'That the sea is the sweat of the earth,' writes Sir Thomas Browne, 'that the serpent before the fall went erect like a man . . . being neither consonant unto reason nor corresponding unto experiment are unto us no axioms.' Scheuchzer creates in the mind of the reader much the same impression of a man who rejects the picturesque with reluctance and believes rather more than half of what he was told. He has, for instance, no hesitation whatever in accepting the fact that dragons still haunt the Alps. His *a priori* reason for this belief is the existence of many caves admirably adapted to their housing needs, and his *a posteriori* reasons are the sworn depositions of many reliable witnesses who have encountered dragons.

'Some *"vir quidam probus"*,' writes Leslie Stephen, 'comes home in the evening with a swimming in the head and a marked uncertainty about the motions of his legs. He attributes these unprecedented phenomena to the influence of the dragon who encountered him in the forest. From his description an accurate portrait of the dragon is composed. The remarkable thing about these diagrams is the singular variety of type in the genus dragon.'

Finally, if there were no dragons, how comes it that the museum at Lucerne contains an undoubted dragon stone? Such stones are admittedly very rare, but this is only because of the exceptional difficulty of securing one. The stone must be cut out of the dragon's head while the dragon is asleep, and if he wakes, not only will the dragon die but the stone itself will miraculously vanish. It is therefore essential not only to scatter soporific herbs during the operation but to use the appropriate incantation. All of which requires an operator who must be, as Scheuchzer admits, unusually skilful and unusually brave. It was therefore providential that the dragon stone in the Lucerne museum was casually dropped by a passing dragon. It is obviously genuine, Scheuchzer argues, because if the peasant who brought it to the museum had been dishonest, he would never have invented so obvious and commonplace an explanation, but would have accounted for its existence by some astounding story such as that the stone had come from the far Indies. Moreover, Scheuchzer insists, the genuineness of this particular stone is proved by the fact that it not only cures haemorrhages but also dysentry.

Scheuchzer was an engaging mixture of credulity and genuine scientific curiosity and achievement. He encouraged, for instance, the monks on the St Gotthard to make regular observations on the weather and he himself recorded many barometric readings to establish the heights of points reached on his mountain journeys. He was also the first to organize expeditions for his pupils to collect mountain flowers and to study the mountain structures.

And there we may take leave of our Zürich professor. 'He is,' as Mr Gribble rightly said, 'no shadow of a name but a real man whom we can know and like—can like all the better, perhaps, because he so often allows us the privilege of a smile at his expense.'

*Gottlieb Sigmund Gruner*
Scheuchzer's successor, Gruner, was perhaps more of a compiler than a traveller, depending both for his matter and also for his illustrations on a number of local correspondents. There was, as Gruner realized, a public eager to read about the mountains. Many of his own countrymen, and many visitors from foreign lands, were visiting the glaciers of Grindelwald and Chamonix. The Pastor at Grindelwald had made a financial success of the inn which he started and later transferred to a peasant landlord.

In the preface to the first edition of his work, published in 1760, Gruner states that his purpose was to describe the Alps in history and nature, and then to discuss their physical structure. According to that distinguished Swiss mountaineer, Bernhard Studer, Gruner's *Die Eisgebirge des Schweizerlandes* (three volumes) rendered a real service to Natural Science in Switzerland, and Studer gives Gruner credit for the first successful attempt to produce a comprehensive survey of the Swiss Alps.[1]

The reception of these three volumes encouraged Gruner to produce in 1778 a popular edition in two volumes under a new

[1] *Physische Geographie der Schweiz.* B. Studer. Berne, Zürich, 1863.

title, *Reisen durch die merkwürdigsten Gegenden Helvetiens.*
The success of this book may be judged by the fact that de
Saussure learned German in order to read it, and paid a generous
tribute to the author in the first volume of his *Voyages.*

# 3

## ALBRECHT VON HALLER
### *The Father of Alpine Ideologists*

———

A FEW months after Waterloo, the Helvetic Society of Science was inaugurated at Geneva. At the end of the banquet the guests joined in singing

> *Emules et jamais rivaux*
> *Ne cherchons que vérités sûres,*
> *Rassemblons dans nos travaux*
> *Plus de faits que conjectures:*
> *Ayons toujours devant les yeux*
> *Haller, Bonnet et de Saussure,*
> *Nous saurons nous montrer comme eux*
> *Les vrais amis de la Nature.*

De Saussure's name will be forever linked with Mont Blanc. Charles Bonnet, a Genevese aristocrat who once enjoyed a great reputation as a philosopher and physiologist, is forgotten, and Haller is only remembered by specialists in the history of man's changing attitude to the mountains.

Albrecht von Haller, the son of a Bernese lawyer, was born in 1708 and died in 1777. Before he was ten, he produced an excellent piece of Greek prose. In later life he had a perfect mastery of English, French and Italian, and could read Greek, Hebrew and Chaldaic. At the early age of sixteen he studied medicine at Tübingen, and took his degree some years later at Leyden. After a visit to London he returned to his native mountains, and wrote a poem, *Die Alpen,* in 1729, which was translated into English, French, Italian and Latin, and ran through thirty editions. A thousand copies of an infinitely greater poem, Wordsworth's *Excursion,* sufficed the British public for thirteen years. Prince Radziwill was so impressed by *Die Alpen* that he sent Haller a commission as Major-General in the Polish Army, which strikes us as funny, but which was perhaps no more irrational than

32

3  MARCH OF THE CONFEDERATES OVER THE ST. GOTTHARD PASS 1509. Coloured miniature from Diebold Schilling's Lucerne Chronicle 1513

4  SCHWYZ WITH MYTHEN. Woodcut from Joh.Stumpf's Chronicle of Switzerland, Zurich 1548

making victorious generals honorary doctors of Oxford or Cambridge.

In 1728 Haller returned to Berne, and practised for some years as a surgeon and physician. In 1736 he made his second long tour of the Alps, in the course of which he visited many valleys in the Oberland which were already well known. He left Berne on his appointment by King George II of England and Hanover to the Chair of Botany, Medicine and Anatomy at the University of Göttingen. His contributions to science still further increased the European reputation which he had achieved by his poem *Die Alpen*. He was elected a Fellow of the Royal Society in 1751 and a Foreign Member of the French Academy in 1754. Frederick the Great vainly attempted to secure his services. 'Haller,' he wrote, 'is the best physiologist in Europe, the greatest botanist in Germany, and at the same time a man of genius. I give you *carte blanche* for Haller. Kings are only too happy when they can get for a little money what all the diamonds in the world cannot purchase.'

Haller returned to Berne and was given a seat on the Council of Two Hundred, a magistracy, the lucrative post of director of the salt mines in Bex, and finally a special appointment with a salary of 1,400 francs a year which, with his other emoluments, made him content to pass the rest of his life in Switzerland.

He continued to spend much time in the mountains in pursuit of his botanical studies, but he was no mountaineer, and never ventured far above the limit of the cow pastures, the 'alps' in the original sense of the term. Indeed, he disliked what he called 'the terrible solitudes' of the remoter and less accessible Valaisian alps. He felt no need to go further afield in search of flowers than Scheidegg, Grimsel, Furka, Gemmi, Stockhorn, Niesen and the Chamossaire above Villars.

Haller was a conservative both in religion and in politics. He was worried by his old friend Bonnet's deviations from the stricter variants of Protestant orthodoxy, and he cordially distrusted Voltaire, a distrust which seems to have amused Voltaire who wrote, 'I shall always find time to assure you of my esteem, and even my love, for I should like you to realize that you are very lovable.' Gibbon, on the other hand thought him far from lovable. 'With all his admirers, Haller has few friends. Wherever he has happened to reside his haughty and ambitious character has offended all his acquaintances.' Some of his acquaintances, perhaps, but Haller had many devoted friends. It may be that his inherent distrust of those who were radicals either in politics or in religion was only partially concealed during his meetings with Gibbon, and if so, he would have been as little disarmed by Gibbon's admiration as he had been by Voltaire's compliments.

'I do not care,' he had written, 'for tolerance as Voltaire offers it to me. These philosophers, no sooner tolerated, would become our persecutors.' And he might perhaps have made a similar comment, had he read the remarkable tribute paid to him in his *Journal* by Gibbon. 'I am little interested in a work on botany, but very much in Mr Haller. This universal genius united the fire of poetry with the sagacity and discernment of the philosopher: his natural abilities are equal to his acquired knowledge. His memory is retentive to a degree almost miraculous.'

But the tribute which would have given him the keenest pleasure was paid to him by de Saussure who confessed that he found it impossible to express the admiration verging on adoration which Haller inspired in him, and who declared that his conversation sparkled not with the fictitious fire which both dazzles and fatigues but with a gentle and deep glow which warms and seems to lift you to the speaker's level. And de Saussure adds that, though Haller could hardly fail to be conscious of his superiority, he never asserted it offensively, but listened with the greatest patience to any objections which might be raised, and cleared up any ambiguities. De Saussure, it is true, admitted that if the question touched on religion or morals, Haller might assume a dictatorial air, and this perhaps explains why Gibbon did not like him. The week which de Saussure passed in his company in 1764 left, so he tells us, an ineffaceable impression on his mind. 'I parted from him with the greatest regret, and only his premature death brought to an end our intimate relations.'

Haller's famous poem was important for two reasons. First, because it was a vigorous reaction against the generally accepted doctrine that mountains were aesthetically unattractive, and secondly because Haller was the first to formulate what may be called an Alpine ideology. Two stanzas, the first of which I shall quote in the original German, the second in Mr Douglas Fresh-

34

field's admirable prose paraphrase, are characteristic of Haller in his attempts to describe mountain scenery.

> *'Wenn Titans erster Strahl der Gipfel Schnee vergüldet*
> *Und sein verklärter Blick die Nebel unterdrückt,*
> *So wird, was die Natur am prächtigsten gebildet,*
> *Mit immer neuer Lust von einem Berg erblickt;*
> *Durch den zerfahrnen Dunst von einer dünnen Wolke*
> *Eröfnet sich zugleich der Schauplatz einer Welt,*
> *Ein weiter Aufenthalt von mehr als einem Volke*
> *Zeight alles auf einmal, was sein Bezirk enthält;*
> *Ein sanfter Schwindel schliesst die allzuschwachen Augen,*
> *Die den zu breiten Kreis nicht durchzustrahlen taugen.'*

And here, for those who do not know German, is Mr Freshfield's paraphrase of stanzas 34-45:

'A medley of mountains, lakes, and rocks presents itself clearly to view, clad in colours which fade gradually as the distance grows. On the horizon shines a crown of gleaming summits; the nearer heights are covered with dark forests. A neighbouring hill stretches out gentle terraces on which feed flocks whose lowings wake the dales. Here a lake spreads its beautiful mirror in the depths of a valley and gives back the quivering light which the sun throws on its ripples. There valleys, carpeted with verdure, open before the eyes and form folds which grow closer as they recede. Elsewhere a bare mountain displays its steep and smooth flanks, while it lifts to the skies the eternal ice, which, like crystal, throws back the sun's rays and dares the attack of the dog-days. Near it a vast and fertile alp supplies abundant pasturages; its gentler slopes glow with the sheen of ripening crops and its hillocks are covered with herds. Climates so opposite are separated only by a narrow vale, where the shade is always fresh.'[1]

This is doubtless an accurate catalogue of things seen, but Haller never wrote a line which I would re-read in those moods of mountain nostalgia when one seeks 'to beget the golden time again'. The technique of word-painting of scenery is only mastered by those who can evoke remembered beauty by the discern-

[1] *The Life of Horace Benedict de Saussure* by Douglas W. Freshfield. Edward-Arnold, London 1920, p. 411.

ing blend of factual record with metaphor, simile and analogy, for as Aristotle said, the mark of a great poet is the skill with which he uses metaphor. Compare, for instance, Haller's

'*Wenn Titans erster Strahl der Gipfel Schnee vergüldet*'
(When the first ray of the Titan gilds the snow peak)

with the famous quatrain of Tennyson's

'How faintly-flush'd, how phantom-fair,
Was Monte Rosa hanging there
A thousand shadowy-pencill'd valleys
And snowy dells in a golden air.'

By the masterly use of metaphor and simile, Tennyson evokes the remembered beauty not of any mountain sunrise but of the unique effect of remoter snows, glowing in the dawn, and 'hanging there' above the shadowy foothills. But it is unfair to compare Haller with Tennyson, and of far greater interest to investigate the reasons for the extraordinary popularity of a mediocre poem.

Haller was fortunate in timing his poem, for the reaction against Renaissance standards of taste had begun, and there were the first signs of lessening appreciation of classical architecture which conformed to the accepted 'recipes for beauty and sublimity', as formulated by writers to whom Vitruvius was the final authority. Mountains were obviously repulsive for, as Thomas Burnet pointed out in 1759, 'there is nothing in Nature more shapeless and ill-figured than an old Rock or Mountain, and all that variety that is among them, is but the various Modes of irregularity'. Burnet, it is true, offers one slight consolation that, however ugly the mountains may be, they cannot be as ugly as 'when they were new born or raw', for, as he justly observes, 'a Ruin that is fresh looks much worse than afterwards'.

When, however, *Die Alpen* appeared, there were many people who suspected that mountains were not as ugly as all that, and who were reassured by the discovery that Haller expressed what they had felt, and thus provided a façade of respectability for what had till then seemed eccentric and even faintly disreputable views.

But it was not only because Haller was almost the first poet of the mountain cult that *Die Alpen* achieved a European reputation, but also and perhaps mainly because Haller was one of the first propagandists of an ideology with explosive but unsuspected possibilities, the ideology which contrasts the simple peasant, uncorrupted by luxury, with the other dwellers on this contaminated planet. From time immemorial, mankind has been haunted by ancestral memories of Paradise lost, and consoled by fugitive hopes of an earthly Paradise regained or rediscovered. Both sentiments are expressed in *Die Alpen*.

Haller introduces this theme with a lament that the Golden Age was so short-lived:

> 'Beglückte goldne Zeit, Geschenk der ersten Güte,
> O dass der Himmel dich so zeitig weggerückt!'

but finds consolation in the belief that the Golden Age still lingered in Alpine valleys:

> 'Ihr Schüler der Natur, Ihr kennet noch goldne Zeiten.'

Pomp and luxury undermine the foundations of the State, but the peasant, uncorrupted by wealth, is content with his lot. He need not fear that the marriage bed will be defiled by sin, for its sentinels are Chastity and Reason:

> 'Hier bleibt das Ehbett rein, man dinget keine Hüter
> Weil Keuschheit und Vernuft darum zu Wache stehn.'

The peasant is untempted by illicit joys; virtuous love does not become stale when consummated:

> Ihr Vorwitz spähet nicht auf unerlaubte Güter,
> Was man geliebet, bleibt auch beym Besitze schön.'

Haller, as a sturdy Protestant, would have rejected with contempt the dogma of the Immaculate Conception, that is, the belief that the Madonna did not inherit of the taint of original sin, but he might have found it difficult to refute the charge that he himself believed in the Immaculate Conception of all good Berglers. Lines such as

37

*'Bey euch, vergnügtes Volk hat nie in den Gemüthern
Der Laster schwarze Brut den ersten Sitz gefasst.'*

are at least tolerant of the interpretation that the true Bergler is
never tempted to sin.

Haller's poem appeared in a transitional period between the
unquestioned acceptance of the Established Order and its revolutionary overthrow in France. There was a receptive public, only
too anxious to welcome any writer who could paint an effective
contrast between a corrupt society and an uncorrupted mountain peasantry. As most of Haller's readers had no first-hand
knowledge either of aristocrats or of peasants, they found it easy
to believe in the corruption of the former and in the virtues of
the latter.

Rousseau, as we shall see, was greatly influenced by *Die Alpen*,
and it was Rousseau who transformed the innocuous sentimen-
talism of Haller's ideology into ideological dynamite. It is indeed
ironic that Haller, a stubborn conservative both in religion and
in politics, should have done so much to give shape and substance
to the ideology which was the inspiration of the French Revolution.

# 4

## ROUSSEAU AND THE MOUNTAIN CULT

----

JEAN-JACQUES ROUSSEAU was born at Geneva on June 28, 1712. Rousseau's ancestors had left Paris for Geneva in 1529 so that Rousseau could claim to belong to an old Genevese family. His childhood was unhappy. 'I cost my mother her life, and my birth was the first of my woes.'

At the age of sixteen he ran away from Geneva and wandered into Savoy, whose dukes had waged for generations unremitting warfare against the political freedom and the Reformed Faith of Geneva. Rousseau was warmly welcomed by M. de Pontverre, the priest of Confignon. He made the best of his opportunities to convert this young fugitive from the citadel of heresy. Rousseau writes:

'He spoke to me of the heresy of Geneva, of the authority of the Holy Mother Church, and gave me dinner. I found little to answer to arguments which ended thus: that I judged priests at whose houses one dined well were at all events worth as much as our ministers. I was too good a guest to be a good theologian, and his Frangi wine, which struck me as excellent, was such a triumphant argument on his side, that I should have blushed to oppose so capital a host.'

Rousseau was received into the Church of Rome, and Mme de Warens, a recent convert who had left her husband in Vevey, assumed the role of his protectress. Meanwhile, Rousseau had his living to make. After a brief and unhappy career as a lackey, he returned to Mme de Warens and lived with her for the next twelve years. Mme de Warens had succumbed to the attractive doctrine preached by a certain de Tavel, who insisted that the importance of sexual relations had been greatly exaggerated, and that *liaisons* were innocent provided that outward decorum was observed. She was therefore persuaded to exchange the maternal for a more intimate role.

In 1741 Rousseau left Mme de Warens for Paris, where he soon made a name for himself as an original and revolutionary writer. During the course of a brief visit to Geneva he rejoined the Church of his baptism and resumed his rights as a citizen.

Meanwhile the authorities at Geneva had begun to read his books, and the more they read them the less they liked them. *Émile* was burnt by the public hangman, and Rousseau himself was forced to fly the country. He crossed the frontier to Switzerland, and tried to settle down in Yverdon, but was promptly expelled by the reactionary Council of Berne. He took refuge in the village of Môtiers, in what was then the Prussian principality, and which is now the Swiss Canton of Neuchâtel, and here he lived for three years. He was admitted to Communion by the pastor, a weak but broadminded man, and for some time was left in comparative peace, but the echoes of his revolutionary reputation soon penetrated to this peaceful Jurassian village. The villagers of Môtiers disapproved of the Armenian costume which Rousseau assumed, more for convenience than for display. Some of them delighted in throwing stones at this pseudo-Armenian. Finally the Pastor of Môtiers was induced to summon Rousseau before the village consistory in order that he might satisfy them of his orthodoxy. Rousseau duly appeared, and a consistory of illiterate peasants listened gravely while he expounded his faith. They were not impressed, and Rousseau was driven from Môtiers. He took refuge for some time in the charming little isle of St Peter, now virtually a pensinsula, in the Lake of Bienne. But before long he was again discovered and hunted from his retreat by the magistrates of Berne. He took refuge in England, and eventually ended his days in France. He died in 1778, and his body rests beside that of Voltaire in the Panthéon.

Genius evades classification. It is impossible to fit Rousseau into a tidy little ethical category. Certainly no man has recorded with more pitiless sincerity his own faults and failures. In his famous *Confessions* he reveals not only the more picturesque vices which a Cellini might confess with a touch of defiant swagger, but acts of incredible meanness which few men would care to recall.

The man who urged fashionable ladies to suckle their own

young, and who recalled his contemporaries to the high duties of parenthood, deposited his own five children in a Foundlings' Hospital, an action which provoked Burke's famous epigram— 'a lover of his kind and a hater of his kindred. . . . Benevolence to the whole species and want of feeling for every individual with whom the professors come into contact, form the characteristic of the new philosophy.'

## The Proto-Socialist

Rousseau provided Socialism with its charter, and the necessary inspiration for those whose faith was to be tested in the fire of persecution. Rousseau however never equated generous sentiments and generous deeds, and has no responsibility for the comforting theory that you can prove your disinterestedness by abusing the rich rather than by giving your own money to the poor. 'Nobody,' he wrote to a correspondent who had attacked the wealthy, 'has any right to despise the rich until he himself is so prudent and thrifty as to have no need of riches.' In four words Rousseau summed up the essence of *disinterested* philanthropy—*Qui suaded sua det.* ('Let him who persuades others to give, give himself.')

Rousseau's financial integrity was absolute. He preserved his independence by steadfastly and even churlishly refusing to accept gifts from his rich friends or pensions from kings. He lived and he died a poor man.

The man who could write without envy of the rich was unsparing in his condemnation of a system which doomed so many to grinding poverty. The man who had known the indignities of menial service, who had been hungry and homeless, who had seen the wrongs of the poor from within and not from without, had learnt to discover 'the goodness of humanity under its coarser aspect, and who had never tried to shut out these things from his memory', was well qualified, in Lord Morley's phrase, 'to change the blank practice of the older philosophies into a deadly affair of ball and shell'.[1]

Rousseau made history, but never read it. No great thinker was so little learned. He had no verbal memory. His theories were not based on the patient examination of evidence, for he made no attempt to collate the facts of history. He spun out his

[1] *Rousseau* by Viscount Morley. Macmillan.

social theories from premises based on his own emotional re-actions to the world at large. He was fascinated by words, by the subtle play of verbal deductions. His *Contrat Social* was based on the theory that man was born everywhere free, but is every-where in chains, that the golden age lay in the past, and that civilization was a retrogressive movement. His basic theory is demonstrably false, nor did Rousseau ever trouble to justify his first great premise by the slightest shred of evidence, and yet few men have had a profounder influence on contemporary thought.

'Without Rousseau,' said Napoleon, 'France would never have had her Revolution.'

It was from Rousseau that the French Revolutionaries borrowed their conception of the sovereignty of the people. It was from Rousseau's books that they derived the dynamic doc-trine of 'Liberty, Equality and Fraternity'.

Rousseau in his *Discourse on the Origin of Inequality* has drawn a gloomy contrast between man in his primitive state of nature and man as degraded by civilization. He sent this *Dis-course* to Voltaire, Rousseau's great rival in the world of eighteenth-century thought, and Voltaire replied:

'I have received your new book against the human race, and thank you for it. Never was such cleverness used to prove us all stupid. One longs, in reading your book, to walk on all fours. But as I have lost that habit for more than sixty years, I feel, unhappily, the impossibility of resuming it.'

Rousseau and Voltaire were the great architects of the New France, but they worked on parallel lines which never met. They suggest the eighteenth-century contrast between sensibility and sense. Rousseau appealed to the emotions, Voltaire to the mind. Rousseau tried to mobilize the idealists for his campaign against the abuses of the old system. He appealed to men's highest in-stincts. Voltaire fought his enemies with the sword of laughter and the rapier of scorn. Rousseau read little and remembered less. Voltaire had an encyclopaedic thirst for knowledge. Rousseau was essentially religious, Voltaire irreligious. Rousseau had no sense of humour, Voltaire was one of the greatest wits that ever lived. 'The gaiety of Voltaire saddens,' wrote Lord Morley, 'while the sadness of Rousseau consoles.'

### The crime of setting up mountains as objects of human worship

'If Rousseau were tried,' writes Leslie Stephen, 'for the crime of setting up mountains as objects of human worship, he would be convicted by any impartial jury. He was aided, it is true, by accomplices, none of whom were more conspicuous than de Saussure.'

The judge, in passing sentence, would however give due consideration to the fact that Rousseau himself was never converted to the faith which he preached with such success. Rousseau, as we have seen, had been greatly influenced by Haller's poem, *Die Alpen*, but whereas Haller had a real feeling for mountains, Rousseau was only interested in mountains in so far as they could be exploited in the interests of his ideology. Haller returned again and again to the Alpine valleys and to the middle heights, such as the Scheidegg, Rousseau crossed the Simplon like other travellers because it was the least inconvenient route between Italy and Switzerland, but only once ventured into a mountain valley, and even that solitary exception is doubtful, for Bourrit is our only authority for Rousseau's alleged visit to the Turtmantal, and Freshfield tells us that the members of the Rousseau Society at Geneva tended to reject Bourrit's story. None the less the publication of Rousseau's *Nouvelle Héloïse* in 1760 made many converts to the ideological cult of Nature in general and of mountains in particular, but Rousseau's disciples, like their master, made no attempt to explore mountain valleys, whereas de Saussure's *Voyages* sent many readers into the mountains and helped to create Alpine literature.

Professor Philippe Godet of Neuchâtel, whose work *Histoire Littéraire de la Suisse Française* was crowned by the French Académie de Lettres, drew a discerning comparison between Rousseau and de Saussure. 'Rousseau,' he writes, 'had made his mark as a man of letters and a describer of scenery, but in his description he had never risen above the middle zone of our country. With de Saussure, the point of view is enlarged—the High Alps become the central object of his studies; he creates Alpine literature; before him men talked about the sublime horrors of regions of which they knew nothing. From the date of the publication of his *Voyages* the horrors disappeared, the sublimity was better appreciated, descriptions in volumes inspired by the Alps became as numerous as the pictures of which their

13

landscapes furnished the motives. By climbing Mont Blanc the Genevese writer opened a new path to the human spirit; a domain of which Science, Art and Letters are still far from having exhausted the riches.'

Whereas for de Saussure 'the High Alps became the central object of his studies', Rousseau was only interested in the mountains of ideology. The idealization of man in a state of nature led by a natural transition to an idealization of the Alpine peasant and thence to the idealization of life in Alpine valleys. Rousseau's encounters with Alpine peasants were as infrequent as those of Housman with Shropshire lads, and his real sentiments about mountains emerge in the contrast which his hero St Preux implies between the charming and luxuriant Pays de Vaud shores of Lake Leman and the barren heights which rise from the Savoy shore.

Dr Claire Engel, in her interesting work *La Littérature Alpestre en France et en Angleterre aux xviii et xix siècles*, contrasts the English and French contributions to the early literature of Swiss travel, and she attributes the poor quality of the early French Alpine literature to the influence of Rousseau. The English travellers, Archdeacon Coxe, for instance, or Gilbert Burnet, Bishop of Salisbury, or Addison, travelled through Switzerland as genuine observers, their observations on the Swiss being inductions from what they saw and heard rather than deductions from preconceived views about the ennobling influence of primitive surroundings on Alpine peasants. The French, on the other hand, in so far as they were disciples of Rousseau, were not in the least interested in the real Swiss, but only in the imaginary survivors of a mythical Golden Age, living lives of uncorrupted simplicity among the Swiss mountains. The *Nouvelle Héloïse*, as Dr Engel rightly insists, served these travellers 'as a substitute for inspiration and imagination'. Like their master Rousseau, these ideological tourists did not really look at the scenery. Rousseau was born in Geneva, but in none of his writings does he mention the enchanting view of Mont Blanc from Geneva. He spent a great deal of time at Vevey but never refers to the Dent du Midi. He knew Maggiore, but never alludes to Monte Rosa which is visible from the southern reaches of the lake. Rousseau, as Dr Engel remarks, 'neither knew nor loved the Alps'.

# 5

## THE MOUNTAIN ART OF THE
## SWISS KLEINMEISTERS

THE AESTHETIC revolution which discovered beauty in mountains was the work not only of Swiss writers such as Gesner and
Haller, but also of Swiss artists such as Aberli and the Lorys,
father and son, artists of the school which is now known as the
*Schweizer Kleinmeister*. 'Minor artists' would be an incorrect
translation, for the term is applied to a school of Swiss artists
who flourished in the eighteenth and early nineteenth centuries
and was so called not because they were regarded as minor artists,
but because the paintings and engravings which they produced
were small. *Kleinmeister* is, in effect, the Swiss equivalent of
*pittori minori*. As there is no English equivalent for *Kleinmeister*
I have adopted the word and given it its plural, the English form
'Kleinmeisters'.

Few painters before the eighteenth century were interested in
mountain scenery. Mountains often appear in medieval paintings
because the scriptural scene depicted took place in or near a
mountain, but the formal and conventional rocks in the works of
Ghirlandaio, Pesellino or Mantegna reveal as little genuine appreciation of mountain scenery as Dante's mountain epithets, *erto*,
steep, or *duro*, hard, or *rotto*, broken.

None the less there were some artists who revealed in their
work a genuine appreciation of mountains. An artist who had no
feeling for mountain beauty could not have painted Konrad
Witz' 'The Miraculous Draught of Fishes', the setting for which
is not Galilee but Geneva, with Mont Blanc and the Dôle in
background, or the enchanting mountain background of Hubert
Van Eyck's 'Crucifixion', now in the Metropolitan Museum in
New York.

The mountainscapes in works such as Scheuchzer's are pure
fantasy, but in the admirable woodcuts which illustrate Stumpf's
*Chronik* (1548) there are some in which a real attempt has been

made to reproduce a particular mountain with some fidelity. The woodcut of the Mythen behind Schwyz, which we reproduce, marks a real advance in mountain art. The name or names of the wood engravers who illustrated Stumpf's *Chronik* are unknown, but it is probable that Hans Asper, a pupil of the Holbein school, was one of them. Between Stumpf (1548) and Merian (1654), mountain art stagnated. The engraving of Schwyz and the Mythen in Matthaeus Merian's *Topographia Helvetiae, Rhaetiae et Vallesiae* (Frankfurt a. Main 1654) is far inferior to the engraving of the same scene in Stumpf's *Chronik*. Merian was not sufficiently interested in mountains to depict them with the same fidelity with which he depicted towns. His book is a valuable social document because of the accuracy with which he reproduced the appearance of the Swiss towns at the end of the seventeenth century, but he made no real contribution to mountain art.

Though the Swiss mountains had failed to inspire the Swiss painters, both art and architecture flourished in medieval Switzerland under the patronage of the Church. Even where the exterior of a church was plain, the interior was enriched by painting, wood-carving and sculpture. New patrons of art appeared after the Reformation, such as cantonal or municipal governments and wealthy patricians. The Swiss aristocrats who raised and commanded the regiments which entered the service of the kings of France helped to create in Switzerland a fashion for the secular art in which the French excelled. Many patricians had their portraits painted by French artists.

The French painters who depicted pastoral life in terms of romantic shepherds and graceful country festivals, might charm the courtiers of Versailles who had lost touch with reality, only to discover it later on the guillotine, but had few admirers among the more realistic Swiss, most of whom were in a position to contrast pastoral life in French art with pastoral life as they knew it in Switzerland, and it is significant, as Walter Hugelshofer points out,[1] that the Swiss who painted pastoral scenes in the French style found most of their clients outside Switzerland

The development of the Kleinmeister school of mountain

[1] *Schweizer Kleinmeister* by Walter Hugelshofer, Zürich 1945. This album with an excellent introduction contains 104 examples of the best work of the Swiss Kleinmeisters.

artists was the direct result of that mountain cult which Haller had helped to create by his poem *Die Alpen*. Partly as a result of that poem there was a rapid increase in the number of travellers for whom Switzerland was not a mere country of transit, from which they escaped as soon as possible into Italy, but the Mecca of the new mountain cult, to be visited for its own sake. This new fashion in travel created a demand for pictures of the mountains and lakes which the travellers had visited, a demand which the Kleinmeisters hastened to supply. Eighteenth-century Berne, partly because of its ties with France, was not only the social but also the intellectual centre of Switzerland, and Berne, because it was so near to the Oberland lakes and valleys which were increasingly popular with visitors, inevitably became the most important centre of this new school of mountain artists.

Johann Ludwig Aberli (1723-1786) was for many years the acknowledged leader of the Kleinmeisters who settled in Berne. After studying with Heinrich Meyer in Winterthur and with Johann Grimm in Berne, he opened his own school of painting in Berne, among his pupils being J. J. Biedermann and Heinrich Rieter. In a letter to the etcher Adrian Zingg, he wrote enthusiastically of the immense variety of Swiss scenery and the contrast between the awe-inspiring splendour of the peaks and the smiling plains which in places reminded him of Holland. 'Thus I have found myself on my journey exclaiming: Salvator Rosa! Poussin! Savari! Ruysdael or Claude! according as the scenes we saw recalled the manner and choice of subjects of one or other of these great masters.' Aberli helped to create a new type of Alpine painting.

Aberli began as a water colourist, but soon found it impossible to meet the demand for Swiss paintings by the ever-increasing number of travellers. The coloured print was the obvious solution, and Aberli inaugurated the *Umriss-Stich*, which began as an etching in which only the main lines were lightly etched into the plate and the etching was then coloured by hand. Many were coloured by the etcher himself, and these served as models for the craftsmen whom he employed. The result was a compromise between an original painting and modern coloured prints on which print and colour are reproduced mechanically. Other engraving media, such as aquatint and lithograph, came into fashion later.

Caspar Wolf (1735-1783) was Aberli's junior by eleven years. Many of his mountain paintings conformed to the convention of a period when travellers, to borrow Ruskin's dichotomy, were more impressed by the mountain gloom than by the mountain glory. But Wolf did not only paint awe-inspiring precipices, terrifying gorges and the majestic violence of mountain tempests. He also painted a charming series of scenes on the lakes of Thun and Brienz, paintings which Descourtis engraved. In 1776 Wolf made a notable contribution to an album of Oberland etchings, published in Berne, *Merkwürdige Prospekte aus den Schweizer Gebürgen*. The text was the work of Wyttenbach, the author of one of the first guide books to Switzerland, *Manuel pour les savants et les curieux qui voyagent en Suisse* (1786), but what gave the book its real importance was the fact that Haller wrote the preface, the last thing which Haller published. In this preface Haller remarked that he was often asked to write such introductions, which he usually did with reluctance, for it was not always easy to be sincere without wounding the author, but he was delighted to introduce the work of Caspar Wolf, which he greatly admired and which was indeed one of the first attempts faithfully to reproduce mountain scenes. Haller must be given credit for using his great prestige to encourage the new school of mountain artists.

Salomon Gessner (1730-1788) was not only a painter but also a writer. He wrote pastoral idylls which he illustrated. He was an engraver and a painter in tempera. Most of his mountain pictures were of imaginary scenes, and only a few of particular and recognizable scenes, such as the tempera painting of the Reichenbach falls above Meiringen which is reproduced in this book.

### The Lorys

There can be few, if any, private collections of Swiss prints in which the Lorys, father and son, are not represented, for they were among the most prolific and most popular of the Kleinmeisters.

Gabriel Lory père (1763-1840) was born in Berne, at that time the most prosperous town in the old Confederation. Its paternal government—for there was nothing democratic about eighteenth-century Berne—made notable contributions to the city architecture. Relations with France were cordial, and many of the leading

Abbildung des Gletschers im Grindelwaldt in der Herschafft Bern.

5  GRINDELWALD GLACIER. Copper engraving from Matthäus Merian's Topographia Helvetiae, Frankfurt a.M. 1642

6  RHONE GLACIER. Copper engraving by Joh. Melchior Füssli from Joh. Jacob
Scheuchzer's «Naturgeschichten des Schweizerlandes», Zurich 1706/08

Bernese artists and architects resided for some time in Paris and profited by their experience on their return home. Nicolas Sprüngli was one of the architects whose stay in Paris was financed by the Bernese Government, and on his return he built the Hôtel de Musique and the Poste de Police. In both buildings the French influence can be seen. Aberli was yet another Bernese artist who had spent some months in Paris, in 1759, and was greatly influenced by one of the more remarkable of the Bernese painters, Sigmund Freudenberger (1745-1801), who lived for eight years in Paris and was much esteemed by the contemporary French artists.

Gabriel Lory began as a pupil of Wolf and Aberli, and then took up residence in Geneva, where he was employed to colour prints of Chamonix. It was at Geneva that he adopted the French form 'Lory' of his father's name Lohri. After his return to Berne he married the sister of Bartholomé Fehr, a publisher and a dealer in prints, who became one of his patrons. In the Kunstmuseum at Berne there is a water colour by Lory of artists at work colouring prints in his brother-in-law's atelier. Meanwhile, Lory's work benefited from his friendly contacts with Aberli, Freudenberger and Rieter, but his vision of nature in general and mountains in particular was not derivative but personal. Mandach, in his discerning study of the Lorys, father and son,[1] suggests that his taste for elegance had developed during his stay in French Switzerland. As to his method, de Mandach writes, '*Il consiste uniquement à marquer à l'eau-forte les contours de ses modèles. Le reste est réservé au travail sur les épreuves.*'

The Oberland was at first the main scene of his activity. In the first collection which he published he collaborated with Lafond (1763-1831) and later with Karl Zehender (1751-1814) and Johann Jakob Biedermann (1763-1830). Lory, Lafond and Zehender wandered through the Oberland to the lakes of Lucerne and Lowerz in search of mountain subjects. The results were duly published in *Recueil de paysages Suisses* (1797).

Shortly after this book was published, Lory received an unusual commission. The fame of Aberli's coloured prints had reached the Tsar Paul I, who decided that the same method of popularizing Switzerland and advertising its beauties might profitably be exploited on behalf of St Petersburg and Moscow. Lory was there-

[1] Conrad de Mandach, *Deux Peintres Suisses, Les Lory*. Lausanne 1920.

fore commissioned by the Tsar's agent, Jean Walser, to supervise the production of a series of prints based on the paintings of Mayer. Lory accordingly settled at Herisau with his nephew, Friedrich Wilhelm Moritz (1783-1855), one of the most attractive of the Kleinmeisters, who later became the teacher of the famous Swiss artist of the nineteenth century, Albert Anker.

Meanwhile, the 'liberation' of Switzerland by the armies of revolutionary France had begun. The artists who were working for Lory often made sketches in the surrounding country, a practice which was viewed with ever deepening suspicion by the peasants. Perhaps the artists were spies sketching the countryside to assist the invaders? The peasants threatened to throw the artists into the lake of Säntis, and one or two artists were even arrested. Their position became intolerable when the French invaders approached Herisau, and they therefore retreated before the invaders arrived. The general in command of Herisau threatened to treat Lory and his friends as emigrants unless they returned, so return they did, in time to find the revolution triumphant and trees of liberty planted in the main square. Lory, like de Saussure, succumbed to the fleeting but recurring illusion that Utopia can be attained by revolutionary violence and collective action, and when this illusion evaporated, Lory and his colleagues retreated to Lindau in order not to lose all contacts with Russia. The assassination of Paul I on March 23, 1801, brought these particular activities to an end. The views of Russia engraved and coloured by Lory were safely transported to Russia, only to perish in the famous fire of 1812. Fortunately, Lory had kept a selection of prints for his own use, and these are now in the museum at Berne.

In 1805, Lory settled in Neuchâtel to work for the publisher Osterwald, who commissioned him to produce a book of coloured prints to illustrate the different aspects of the road across the Simplon which Napoleon was then building and which was completed in 1807. Many a struggling artist profited by the generosity of Osterwald, who lost a fortune in his publishing business. The *Voyages Pittoresque de Genève à Milan par le Simplon*, one of my most treasured possessions, was eventually published by P. Didot l'ainé in Paris in 1811. Of the thirty-five views, only ten are by Lory père, those of the shores of Lake Leman, some scenes in the Valais, the *grand galerie* and a bridge on the actual Simplon road. The rest are by Lory's far more gifted son. The Simplon series represents the first venture of Lory and son in the medium of the coloured aquatint.

Lory played an active role in the artistic life of Berne. He was a regular exhibitor at the exhibitions which were frequently held in Berne, and he was one of the founders of the Society of Bernese Artists. He died after a short illness in 1840.

Lory's life was not uniformly happy. There was a touch of the misanthrope about him. The son of the *voiturier* sometimes gave offence by a manner which may have been the result of an inferiority complex. Often, we are told by his biographer, he failed to pay the kind of visit or write the kind of letter which would have been helpful in his career.

Gabriel Lory fils (1784-1846) never suffered from the social inhibitions which plagued his father, perhaps because from the first he enjoyed many natural advantages. He was exceptionally good-looking and generously endowed with charm, and was at ease in all the social strata from aristocrats to mountain peasants. In the Kunstmuseum at Berne there are two drawings by Gabriel Lory of himself and his father in which the artist has unwittingly revealed the contrast between father and son, for the self-portrait is the portrait of a man who has nothing to fear from society, whereas his father's expression is distrustful, as if he still felt socially insecure.

The younger Lory's greatest friend was a member of an aristocratic Neuchâtel family, the de Meurons. Maximilien de Meuron (1785-1868), Lory's junior by one year, had abandoned a diplomatic career to paint. His painting of the Eiger, in the Museum of Neuchâtel, was greatly over-praised by Rodolphe Töpffer, who described it as 'le point de départ de la peinture alpestre', a grotesque misstatement. De Meuron seems to have been discouraged by his comparative lack of success as an artist, and he devoted the rest of his life to creating a public for young artists rather than to creating works of art himself. He founded the Neuchâtel Art Museum, and his home became a centre for Neuchâtel artists. His son, Albert de Meuron, made a greater name as a mountain painter. One of his more attractive works, 'Le Matin dans les Alpes', hangs in the Geneva museum.

Lory was just twenty when he first met de Meuron, and twenty-two when he and de Meuron made the first of their three Italian journeys together. In 1809 they crossed the Simplon to Milan, a journey in the course of which Lory made the sketches for the Simplon collection of aquatints. In 1811 Lory rejoined his friend in Rome, and it is to this journey that we owe the delightful water colours of Rome and Naples, now in the Berne Kunstmuseum. In 1812 Lory married the daughter of Henri de Meuron, presumably a kinsman of his great friend, and a captain of the Swiss regiment of de Meuron which was in the service of the Dutch East Indies and of England. Gabriel Lory was even more productive than his father. His best-known books of prints were *Costumes Suisses* (1824), in which he collaborated with F. W. Moritz (1785-1855), *Voyage Pittoresque de l'Oberland Bernois* (1822) and *Souvenirs de la Suisse* (1829), to both of which his father contributed.

It was Lory's practice to colour one print, which was carefully preserved and served as a model for the craftsmen who were employed to colour the remaining prints.

The older Lory only left Switzerland when the French occupied his country, but the younger Lory was a great traveller, and visited Italy, France and England. He died suddenly of a heart attack, in the presence of de Meuron, who had been dining with him. Lory complained of palpitations, and his wife left the room to summon a doctor. Before she could return, he had died in the arms of his greatest friend.

Conrad de Mandach's *Deux Peintres Suisses*, which is my principal authority for the Lorys, is very fully illustrated. Perhaps the best collection of the Swiss mountain prints is the collection made by the late R. W. Lloyd, which he bequeathed to the British Museum and which can be seen by anybody with a card for the Print Room, obtainable on application to the Museum.

It is impossible, within the limits of a chapter, to do justice to the many Kleinmeisters who deserve more than a passing mention, to Heinrich Rieter (1751-1818), for instance, who is generally regarded as the successor of Aberli, and who was perhaps at his best in his studies of Swiss lakes, his watercolour, for instance, of Lake Léman near Lausanne, his charming oil painting of Lake Thun, or his oil painting of Iseltwald on Lake Brienz, all of which are in private collections and only known to me in reproductions. The painting of Iseltwald reminds me of the nostalgic dreams which gave me momentary consolation during the long war years of exile from the Alps.

There was always a moment in the dream when I tried hard to persuade myself that a displaced mountain was not really displaced, that you *could*, for instance, see the Jungfrau from Zweilutschinen, and then, of course, I awoke. In the background of Rieter's Iseltwald the Jungfrau rises above mists just to the left of the Niesen. Unfortunately the Jungfrau is invisible from Iseltwald.

Among the many other Kleinmeisters to whose mountain art I should attempt to do justice if I were writing not a chapter but a book, may be mentioned Peter Birmann (1758-1844), W. A. Toepffer (1765-1847), B. A. Dunker (1746-1807), Samuel Birmann (1793-1847), son of Peter Birmann, Marquart Wocher (1758-1830), whose panorama from Thun (1816) was his best-known work, Sigmund Freudenberger (1745-1801), whose influence on Lory père has already been mentioned, J. J. Meyer (1787-1858), who was at one time associated with the Lorys, and J. B. Isenring (1796-1860), a master of etching and one of the first to make experiments in what was then the new art of landscape photography.

## The Final Phase

The pioneers of the Kleinmeister school were self-employed artists who coloured their own prints and whose work was an attempt to interpret their own ideas, but the self-employed artist gradually disappeared as more and more of the Kleinmeisters found themselves working for publishers such as Wagner in Berne, Fehr in St Gallen or Walser in Herisau. These publishers were sensitive to the demands of the travelling public and ambitious to provide what their clients wanted. The creative inspiration of the artist, as Walter Hugelshofer points out, had to yield to the commercial demands of his employer, with the result that the new work could not stand comparison with the old. The inevitable decline of the Kleinmeister school began in the early decades of the nineteenth century, and the end came before 1850. The Kleinmeisters were succeeded by ambitious painters, some of whom, notably Calame and Hodler, achieved European fame as mountain artists, but their influence on mountain appreciation was incomparably less than that of the Kleinmeisters. The aesthetic revolution, which created the mountain cult, had triumphed before Calame began to paint, whereas the coloured prints of the Kleinmeisters, proudly exhibited by the traveller returned from Switzerland, must have awakened a feeling for mountain beauty in many of their friends and inspired them to visit the scenes which Aberli or Wolf had depicted. The influence of the Swiss Kleinmeisters in this respect was far greater than that of William Pars, whose Swiss drawings, exhibited in 1771 in London, are described by Mr Laurence Binyon as 'perhaps the earliest revelation of the high Alps to the untravelled Englishman', and probably even greater than that of John Robert Cozens and Francis Towne.[1]

It is not my purpose to arrange Swiss mountain artists in an order of merit, and I admit that my own preference for the Kleinmeisters, whose works hang in our sitting room at home, is influenced by other than aesthetic considerations, but there are two impersonal points which may be fairly made. The Kleinmeisters created a school, and this cannot be claimed for the Swiss mountain artists of the nineteenth century. Secondly, the Kleinmeisters were recognized as outstanding practitioners of this particular genre in mountain art, but no one could make a similar claim on behalf of the Swiss mountain artists of the nineteenth century, for the greatest mountain artist of that century was not a Swiss but an Italian, Segantini.

## The Charm of the Kleinmeisters

To those who love mountains, 'features of a landscape' is something more than a metaphor. To attribute personality to inanimate rock and ice is to be guilty of what Ruskin calls 'the pathetic fallacy', and yet the mountains 'to which, in spite of all reason', as the agnostic Leslie Stephen confessed, 'it is impossible not to attribute some shadowy personality', continue to provide examples in Alpine literature of the pathetic fallacy. The mountain lover for whom each peak has its own 'shadowy personality'

[1] I have written at greater length about mountain art in general in Chapters II and VI of *Switzerland and the English*, which contains reproductions of the mountain art of Lory, Pars, Cozens, Towne, Turner, Ruskin, Sir William Rothenstein, Adrian Allison and Hodler. My book, *A Century of Mountaineering*, is illustrated by coloured reproductions of the mountain paintings of Calame, Hodler, E. T. Compton, J. Brett, A. Gos, G. Giacometti and E. Aufdenblatten.

starts with a bias in favour of the artist who makes some attempt to interpret this personality, and with a bias against the artist for whom an impressionistic and distorted misrepresentation of a mountain is merely a pretext to reveal in paint his own personality. What the mountain lover demands from the artist is not a likeness of the artist but a likeness of the mountain.

Now the cult of personality has never been encouraged in Switzerland, and the art of the Kleinmeisters is as unpretentious as the Swiss character. They practised what Cosimo de Medici preached, for they too believed that the secret of success is to aim at finite ends. They seldom tried to convey the power, might, majesty and dominion of the great peaks, and when they did make this attempt, they failed, but they were eminently successful in suggesting the charm of lakes and cloudless skies and radiant snows. The relationship of their work to the greatest masterpieces of mountain art is, as Sir Gavin de Beer once remarked to me, analogous to that of the minuet to the symphony.

It is, I think, an inescapable deduction from their work that they had a genuine appreciation of mountain beauty. A painter who has no feeling for mountains may find it necessary to introduce them into a painting because the scene depicted took place in or near mountains, but in this case his rocks will be as formal and conventional as rocks in the works of Ghirlandaio and Mantegna, but if he has taken the trouble both to observe and to record with fidelity the structure of a peak, and the subtler effects such as the shadows of moving clouds on snow, it is a reasonable deduction that he was not blind to the beauty which he painted with such care. A mountaineer for whom 'features of the landscape' is not a meaningless metaphor, tends to judge mountain art by the standards of portraiture. He will demand from the mountain artist a likeness of his beloved mountains as faithful as a Titian portrait, and yet, like the Titian portrait, infinitely removed from the prosaic accuracy of a photograph. Dr Claire Engel, in her book *La Litterature Alpestre en France et Angleterre aux XVIII et XIX siècles*, reproduces an aquatint by Linck, a Genevese who began to exhibit his mountain scenes in 1789. The view of the Eiger, Mönch and Jungfrau from Bussalp (not, by the way, from the Scheidegg as stated in this book) combines mountain portraiture with mountain poetry. It is accurate enough for one to identify small details, such as Mac's Leap on the Tschuggen glade ski-run, yet it bears the same relation to a photograph as poetry does to prose. So, too, the younger Gabriel Lory's aquatint of the Wetterhorn from Rosenlaui, a lyrical interpretation of one of the loveliest of Alpine scenes, is at once poetic and yet loyal to objective facts.

The etchings and aquatints of the Kleinmeisters have the exquisite charm of a delightful period piece, the enchanting period just before the smoke-grimed dawn of the Industrial Revolution. In no period of European history was the vandal as destructive as in the nineteenth century. In Lucerne alone he destroyed a house the exterior of which was painted by Holbein, and two-thirds of the old bridge. 'Of the ancient architecture and most expressive beauty of the country,' write Ruskin, 'there is now little vestige left; and it is one of the few reasons which console me for the advance of life, that I am old enough to remember the time when the sweet waves of the Reuss and Limmat (now foul with the refuse of manufacture) were as crystalline as the heaven above them; when her pictured bridges and embattled towers ran unbroken round Lucerne; when the Rhone flowed in deep-green, softly dividing currents round the wooden ramparts of Geneva; and when from the marble roof of the western vault of Milan, I could watch the Rose of Italy flush in the first morning light, before a human foot had sullied its summit.'

The Switzerland of the Lorys was the Switzerland of the Romantic movement, the Switzerland which Ruskin first saw as a boy and mourned in prose whose beauty, alas, is no adequate compensation for the loveliness which the vandals destroyed or for the ugliness which the vandals created.

7 JOH. JACOB SCHEUCHZER (1672–1733), naturalist. Copper engraving by Jos. Nutting after Joh. Melchior Füssli

8  SALOMON GESSNER (1730–1788). Idyllic Alpine landscape. Gouache. (Zürcher Kunstgesellschaft)

Une Partie des Glacières du Grindelwald
Dessiné par J. L. Aberli et gravé par M. Pfenninger avec Privilege.

9 LUDWIG ABERLI (1723–1786). Grindelwald glacier. Coloured copper engraving by M. Pfenninger

10  Ludwig Hess (1760–1800). Klöntal with Glärnisch 1796. Oil. (Zürcher
Kunstgesellschaft)

# 6

## THE GENEVESE

DE LUC, Bourrit, de Saussure and Rousseau were Genevese but not Swiss, for they died before Geneva joined the Swiss Confederation. The Switzerland of their epoch was a confederation of thirteen Cantons—Uri, Schwyz, Unterwalden, Lucerne, Zug, Zürich, Glarus and Berne (together forming the so-called eight old Cantons), and in addition Appenzell, Fribourg, Solothurn, Basel and Schaffhausen. This Confederation ruled over various subject territories and bailiwicks. Morat and Grandson, for instance, were held jointly by Berne and Fribourg. When the armies of revolutionary France invaded Switzerland in 1798, they proclaimed that their noble purpose was to 'liberate' Vaud from the hated rule of Berne.

The Confederation was allied to independent States which subsequently became Swiss Cantons. Geneva, the Valais, the Grisons and Neuchâtel were allied States or, as the Swiss described them, zugewandte Orte. The Confederate Cantons themselves were in effect autonomous States, each of which had its own militia, its own customs and its own currency. The links between a Canton and an allied State might often be closer than between one Canton and another. The links between Protestant Berne and the allied State of Geneva, for instance, were probably stronger than between Protestant Berne and Catholic Schwyz.

Clearly, Placidus a Spescha, who died after the Canton of Grisons joined the Confederation, has every claim to be considered Swiss, and Swiss historians write of the Valais as Swiss even during the centuries when it was only an allied State, and somehow I find it less easy to think of de Saussure or Rousseau as Swiss than the sixteenth-century Cardinal Schiner of Sion, perhaps because even today the Genevese have been less completely assimilated than the Valaisians. I remember putting this point to a member of one of the old patrician families of Geneva.

He seemed to me to think of himself as neither Swiss nor French but solely as a Genevese, the citizen of a Canton which was closely associated, but not identified, with Switzerland. He conceded that this was more or less his own conception of his status.

None the less, the practice of Swiss historians to regard all Genevese as Swiss, irrespective of whether they died before or after Geneva joined the Confederation, seems to me sound, and would appear to be accepted as such by modern Genevese.

### Jean-André de Luc (1727-1817)

Jean-André was the elder son of Jean François de Luc, a Genevese watchmaker and an active member of the Popular Party. He was at one time fairly intimate with Rousseau, who, however, has left on record the fact that he thought him a great bore. He enjoyed the respect of the Radicals, for in 1774 he was appointed to head the delegation of Représentants which congratulated de Saussure on his proposals for education reform.

Jean-André and his brother, Guillaume, inherited their father's political principles which did not, however, prevent Jean-André from enjoying a distinguished public career, for he was a member of diplomatic missions to Paris and Berne, and also a member of the Grand Council of Geneva. None the less, the sound scientific education which he had received provided the main interest of his life. He invented the hygrometer, and his reputation as a meteorologist and inventor proved invaluable when he left Geneva and established himself in England, where he married. He was elected a Fellow of the Royal Society, but the offer of an appointment as Reader to the Queen proved too strong for his radical principles. He is mentioned in Miss Burney's memoirs, and seemed to have been a favourite target for the practical jokes of the Royal Dukes. He died at Windsor at the age of ninety.

It was as a meteorologist that he made a name for himself. His six-volume treatise on geology, designed to reconcile geology and Genesis, was dedicated to the Queen, but there is no evidence that she read it. He combined mountaineering with research, for he seldom neglected to ascertain the temperature at which water would boil at different altitudes. He was one of the first to climb snow and glacier-capped peaks. He made, for instance, with his brother Guillaume, the first ascent of the Buet (3,057 m., 10,291 feet). The summit of the Buet, the highest point in the range to the north of the valley of Chamonix, is a broad glacier-capped plateau. De Luc succeeded on his third attempt, the ascent being made from Sixt on September 22, 1770. After admiring the view, of which he wrote an eloquent description, de Luc observed that the entire party were standing on the edge of a cornice 'which jutted over a frightful precipice. Our first movement,' writes de Luc, 'was a precipitate retreat. But having gathered by reflection that the addition of our own weight to this prodigious mass, which had thus supported itself for ages, counted for absolutely nothing, and could not possibly break it, we laid aside our fears and went back to the terrible terrace.' It was not until many lives had been lost by breaking cornices that climbers began to treat them with due respect.

He made a second ascent in 1772 by a different route. His party spent the night in the valley of Anterne and had some difficulty in finding the chalet where they planned to sleep. At last they found a hut, and the women gathered round a fire immediately made them welcome and offered them milk and cheese, which was all that they had, and also the hospitality of their one and only bedroom, which the men shared with these peasant women without causing or feeling embarrassment. On their return next day they were overtaken by storm and darkness and were rescued by their hostesses, who struggled up the mountain to find them, and succeeded in spite of the fact that it was only the largest of their torches which was not extinguished by rain and wind. Next morning they refused to accept any payment for their services. However, de Luc eventually persuaded the one 'who seemed to be less in the position of a mistress than the other' to accept a crown. 'The idea of accepting payment for a service !'

'It is thus,' writes de Luc, 'that human nature is corrupted; and there are times when I reproach myself. I should reproach myself without ceasing if there were any chance that Anterne would become a frequented place. And this is not merely a passing reflection. I have made it again and again when I have realized that it is thus that one alters the nature of the reward which good people look for.'

De Luc was not the last mountain traveller to suspect that the simplicity of the mountain people would not survive closer contact with visitors from the outer world, but unlike Haller and Rousseau, he did at least offer real evidence, based on personal experience, in support of the doctrine of the uncorrupted mountain peasant.

### Marc-Théodore Bourrit (1735-1819)

Bourrit was by birth a *natif* of Geneva, that is, a plebeian, a fact which certainly influenced his relations with the patrician de Saussure. He had some slight talent as an artist and a fine voice. At an early age he obtained an appointment as Precentor in the Cathedral choir, supplementing his income by painting miniatures. He was twenty-two when he first discovered his passion for the Alps. 'It was,' he writes, 'from the summit of the Voirons that the view of the Alps first awoke in me a desire to become acquainted with them.'

He had made the fortunate discovery that it was easier at Geneva to sell mountain landscapes than portraits. Many of his pictures were sold in England and in Russia, but none of them showed evidence of authentic talent. Though his work is not in the same class as the best of the contemporary Swiss painters, notably Wolf, 'we are often,' writes Douglas Freshfield, 'agreeably surprised at the accuracy of topographical detail attained in such difficult subjects as the chain of Mont Blanc from the Allé Blanche, still more at the power and energy in many of the blotted-in sketches of individual peaks. The rock structure was all-important for de Saussure's purpose,' and it was perhaps this which forced Bourrit to fix his attention on facts and to avoid 'indulgence in the prettiness of which he was far too fond.'

It was his practice to climb in summer and write up his journey in the winter. His *Description des Glacières*, first published in 1773, was translated two years later into English, and went through three English editions. Sir Joshua Reynolds, Horace Walpole and Dr Johnson were among those whose names are to be found in the printed list of subscribers. In 1775, the King of Sardinia received him in Chambéry and gave him a substantial sum of money. In 1779 he visited Paris, and was presented to Louis XVI, who bought his painting of the Oeschinen lake above Kandersteg and granted him a pension of 600 livres on condition that 'he painted two pictures a year for him'. After the Restoration, the pension was renewed by Louis XVIII. Frederick the Great wrote to him and dubbed him 'The Historian of the Alps', a title of which he was inordinately proud. Prince Frederick of Prussia visited him and, after he had heard him describe a sunrise, exclaimed: 'Our Lekain [a famous actor] was ice compared to this man.'

He received his visitors in a house which, so he tells us, 'was embellished with beautiful acacias, planted for the comfort and convenience of strangers who do not wish to leave Geneva without visiting the Historian of the Alps.'

As a historian he had many faults, but he had one redeeming virtue, an unbounded enthusiasm for his subject. His enduring love for the mountains remained the central passion of his life.

As a mountaineer, Bourrit deserved more success than he achieved. He made, in 1775, the first ascent of the Buet from the side of Valorsine. He repeated the expedition six times, convincing evidence of the fact that he did not only climb mountains for prestige. Indeed, one criterion of whether a man climbs for fun or merely to collect peaks in the spirit in which other men collect challenge cups, is his readiness to repeat ascents. The great ambition of his life was to climb Mont Blanc.

In 1785 he and his son joined de Saussure in an attempt on Mont Blanc via the Aiguille du Goûter, but retreated about 600 feet below the summit of the Aiguille. De Saussure, on his return to Geneva, was annoyed by reports which not only greatly exaggerated the perils which they had encountered, but which also attributed the failure of the expedition to his shortcomings as a rock climber. To his protest Bourrit replied, 'I could not but notice that the way you came down was not the happiest. You might have fallen backwards, you might have been hit by the rocks dislodged by the guides, whom you made keep behind you, and we noticed the trouble they had to avoid this.' To offset this offensive attack he enclosed an account of the expedition, praising de Saussure in exaggerated terms. De Saussure found this excessive praise even less to his taste than unjustified criticism. 'No one, perhaps,' he wrote with magnanimity, 'believes more than I do in the kindness and honesty of your heart, but I know very well also that your flighty imagination often makes you see things in a false light. If you could put aside this tendency, there is no reason why you should not keep an agreeable recollection of our excursion. I had every reason to be satisfied with you and your son.'

Meanwhile Bourrit's son, Isaac, had inflicted a foolish and vainglorious letter on de Saussaure. 'Sir,' he wrote, 'you do not envy me my twenty-one years? Who will wonder if a youth of this age, who has nothing to lose, is bolder than a father of a family, a man of forty-six?'

Even this impudent letter could only provoke a gentle retort. 'A moderate amount of boastfulness is no great crime, especially at your age. . . . One may proclaim oneself a little stronger, a little more active than one really is, and yet be the most honest fellow in the world. The truth is that though I recognized in you a slight tendency in this direction, I did not fail to find you very amiable.'

Two years later in his *Voyages*, de Saussure referred to both Bourrits in very friendly terms, but when de Saussure eventually climbed Mont Blanc he made it clear that Bourrit, who had turned up at Chamonix in the hope of acompanying him, could start where and when he wished, provided that he and de Saussure did not start together. Bourrit's last attempt on Mont Blanc in 1788 only just fell short of success. He started with an Englishman, Woodley, and a Dutchman, Camper, but only the Englishman and his guide reached the top. Bourrit abandoned the attempt at the last rocks, about 400 feet below the summit.[1]

The first ascent of Mont Blanc by Dr Paccard, the village doctor of Chamonix, and Jacques Balmat, whom Paccard engaged as a porter, is described in the following chapter. Bourrit would have found it hard to be generous to a man who had achieved what had been the supreme ambition of his life, even if the victor had been de Saussure, the patrician, or a guide, but that Mont Blanc had been climbed by Paccard, an amateur mountaineer and a mere village doctor, was more than Bourrit could bear. Bourrit, as we shall see, was the real originator of the monstrous legend which gave Balmat the credit for having discovered the route and for having led throughout, a legend which was the exact reverse of the truth.

But it was not only in connection with Mont Blanc that Bourrit's vanity and envy distorted his judgment. The amateur who

[1] The initials of Woodley, Camper and Hill are not to be found in the scanty references to their exploits.

forestalled his ambition to be the first traveller to cross the Col du Géant, was relegated to that category of 'unpersons' familiar to all who have read George Orwell's 1984. According to old legends, the passage from Chamonix to Courmayeur over the Col du Géant had been formerly practicable, but its authentic history begins in 1786 when Exchaquet, the director of the mines at Servoz, determined to rediscover the lost pass. Exchaquet was an Alpine pioneer who had explored the lesser summits of the western wing of the Bernese Oberland, and who had all but reached the summit of one of the Aiguilles des Courtes above the Talèfre glacier. In his first attempt he was accompanied by an Englishman, Mr Hill. The attempt failed, but Mr Hill subsequently reached the top of the pass from Courmayeur and returned thence to Courmayeur. He never crossed the pass, though he is credited by Coolidge with having done so, one of the few historical blunders to be found in the works of that erudite historian. In the summer of 1787 Exchaquet, with the guides Marie Couttet and Jean Michel Tournier, left Chamonix at 2.15 a.m. and reached Courmayeur at 8 p.m. on the same day. The weather was fine, and Exchaquet wrote that the party 'met with no difficulties' in the passage of the séracs. On arriving at Courmayeur, they found that John Michel Cachat, who had been originally approached by Exchaquet, and had left him on the eve of the expedition—nominally to look for crystals—had, with his companion Alexis Tournier, anticipated them by twenty-four hours and obtained a certificate of their exploit from the local authorities.

On August 27, 1787, Bourrit set out with his son Charles and four Chamonix guides, including the two men who had behaved so badly to Exchaquet. Whereas Exchaquet had belittled the difficulty of the expedition, Bourrit in his account not only gave a lurid description of the icefall on which Exchaquet 'met with no difficulties', but even suggested that the easy descent to Courmayeur was 'long and difficult' and 'in part dangerous', the 'ridges resembling those of the Aiguille du Goûter'. De Saussure in his own account of the Col du Géant comments on the absence of all difficulties in the descent from the pass to Courmayeur, 'which,' he writes, 'has wrongly been compared to the rocks of the Aiguille du Goûter.' 'This is the only reference,' wrote Freshfield, 'he makes to Bourrit's bombastic narrative. The rebuke thus given, while complete, is in form characteristic of de Saussure's consideration for his former companion.'

But the most objectionable defect in Bourrit's narrative is his failure to make any reference to Exchaquet's previous crossing of the Col. When criticized for this omission, he replied that he had mentioned the two guides who crossed the pass twenty-four hours before Exchaquet, and recognized no obligation to refer to any other predecessor. The fact is that this further offence against the historian's code by the self-styled Historian of the Alps was motivated by the same insane jealousy of any amateur who had enjoyed success, which had inspired his attack on Paccard.

Bourrit was almost as uncritical as Haller in his attitude to the Berglers. He comments in the best Haller-Rousseau manner on the peaceable inhabitants of these solitary valleys, on the innocence of their customs and on the peace which reigns among them. 'Celui qui a jouit,' he wrote, 'd'une satisfaction douce et pure au milieu des paisibles habitantes de ces vallées solitaires, qui a vu l'innocence de leurs moeurs, la tranquille union qui régne dans leur cabanes, la franchise de leurs procédés ne peut facilement l'oublier.' And even Rousseau could not have written with more serene indifference to stubborn facts on the influence of mountains as reconcilers of men of different political parties.

'It is, in fact, the mountains that many men have to thank for their reconciliation with their fellows, and with the human race; and it is there that the rulers of the world and the heads of the nations ought to hold their meetings. Raised thus above the arena of passions and petty interests, and placed more immediately under the influence of Divine inspiration, one would see them descend from these mountains each like a new Moses bringing with them codes of law based upon equity and justice.'

Justice to Paccard? Was this part of the code which Bourrit, the new Moses, brought down from Mont Blanc?

There can be few political vendettas so bitter as those which in Bourrit's time, as in ours, flourish in the shadow of the mountains that Bourrit credits with the power of reconciling men to their fellows.

11  GABRIEL LORY, PÈRE (1763–1840). Lower Grindelwald glacier with Eiger.
Coloured copper engraving

It is only just to add that it was only where his envy was aroused, that Bourrit found it difficult to live at peace with his fellow men. A German, Herr Fischer, who visited him in 1795, declared that 'there is not a character more kind or obliging than Bourrit'. Certainly he could mix on the friendliest terms with mountain lovers irrespective of their religious or political creeds. He did full justice to Murith, the Prior of the St Bernard Hospice, and seems to have been on terms of intimate friendship with this distinguished Catholic climber. His reputation among Catholics must have stood high, for he persuaded the Bishop of Annecy to dispense mountaineers from the obligation to fast in Lent.

When the revolutionary tide swept over Geneva, and the patricians lost power, and in some cases not only power but their lives, Bourrit, born a *natif*, and never admitted to patrician society, found himself suddenly promoted to a leading position in public life. In Geneva and in Paris the revolution was hostile not only to the aristocracy but also to the clergy. It was therefore greatly to the credit of the old Cathedral Precentor that he had the courage to resist the proposal to exclude the clergy from any share in popular education, and to oppose the ridiculous attempt to rename the churches, to rededicate, for instance, one of them to Reason. 'What greatly amused me,' wrote a violent demagogue, 'was to hear a philosopher (de Saussure) praising the Saints, while a simple artisan (Fol) denounced them.'

Bourrit lived to the age of eighty. His love for the mountains was the central passion of his life. He was, as Sir Gavin de Beer remarks, 'one of the first writers to find something to say about the Alps other than that they were high or beautiful'. The pluck and pertinacity which he displayed in his determination to become a climber did him great credit. He made many converts by his writings, and rendered great services by his guide books to Chamonix. His attack on Paccard was disgraceful, but there is enough on the credit side to entitle him to a definite place among the pioneers of the Alps.

## DE SAUSSURE AND MONT BLANC

HORACE BENEDICT DE SAUSSURE was by birth a member of one of the leading families of Geneva. He was born at Conches on February 17, 1740, and until he married at the age of twenty-five, he spent most of his life in the country properties belonging to the family, Conches, Frontenex, the principal de Saussure estate, and Genthod where, so he tells us, he spent the happiest days of his early life.

'I have had from childhood,' he wrote in his *Voyages*, 'the most positive passion for the pleasures of the mountains. I still remember the sensation I felt when, for the first time, my hands touched the rocks of the Salève and my eyes enjoyed its points of view.'

We are indebted to Rousseau, a Genevese by birth, for an entertaining description of eighteenth-century Geneva.

'While a Frenchman writes as he talks, these Genevese talk as they write; they lecture in place of conversing; they give one the impression that they always want to argue. . . . In short, their conversation is sustained, their speeches are harangues, and they gossip with a pulpit air. The Frenchman reads much, but nothing but new books, or rather he runs through them more to be able to say he has read them than for their own sake. The Genevese reads only good books—he reads them to digest them; he does not criticize them, but he knows them by heart. Women as well as men are given to books. It needs all the good sense of the men, all the gaiety of the women, and all the talent both sexes have in common to overcome in the men a touch of pedantry and in the women of preciosity.'

Sumptuary laws were still enforced by the Chambre de la Réformation which survived until 1770. Ladies might not carry watches pinned to their breast. Carriages might only be used for country drives. A bride was expected to walk to church, and might not receive wedding presents. The Chamber further enacted how many guests might be entertained and how many courses might be offered. Monuments and inscribed tombstones were forbidden, and long after the Chamber had ceased to function, it would seem that tombstones were still regarded as 'articles of luxury' inconsistent with the Calvinistic outlook of the city. This at least is the explanation suggested by Mr Freshfield for for the fact that the last resting place of one of Geneva's most famous sons remains uncertain and without record.

Two men profoundly influenced de Saussure's early life and career, his maternal uncle, Charles Bonnet, a scientist of European reputation, and the famous botanist and poet, Albrecht von Haller. It was at Bex, where de Saussure's mother was taking the waters, that de Saussure first met Haller. De Saussure's tribute to Haller has already been quoted in Chapter 3.

In 1762 de Saussure was appointed to the Professorship of Philosophy in the Academy. This title, as understood in Geneva, included not only psychology, logic, morals and divinity, but also the natural sciences. Three years later, de Saussure married Mlle Albertine Amélie Boissier, a member of a prosperous family of bankers. It was his wife's parents who provided the town house, deemed the finest in Geneva, in which he spent most of his life.

The years 1768-69 were dedicated to the Grand Tour, in the course of which the de Saussures visited France, England, Holland and Italy. De Saussure seems to have detected symptoms of unrest beneath the apparent stability of Parisian life, and there is an echo, perhaps unconscious, of Aristotle's belief that it is human nature rather than political systems which are mainly responsible for our troubles in the prescient letter which he wrote to Haller on May 13, 1767.

'There is all over Europe a fermentation which aims at liberty, but of which the sequel in many instances must be a redoubling of slavery. An imperfect philosophy produces aspirations to a liberty without limits; a more perfect philosophy, grounded on experience, will show that the tomb of liberty may be found in the cradle of democracy.'

When de Saussure wrote this letter, seven years had passed since he had taken the first step to arouse the interest of the Chamonix guides in Mont Blanc, but it was not until many years later that the reward which he had offered was claimed by Jacques Balmat.

## The first ascent of Mont Blanc

Mont Blanc is not in Switzerland, and the first men to climb the mountains were not Swiss, but the Swiss, for what seem to me valid reasons, claim de Saussure and Bourrit, though both died before Geneva joined the Swiss Confederation. It is impossible to discuss the place of these eminent Genevese in the history of mountaineering if we ignore what was the most vulnerable aspect of their respective Alpine careers, their deplorable attitude to Paccard, the undoubted initiator of the first successful ascent.

De Saussure must be given the credit for being indirectly responsible for most of the earlier attempts on Mont Blanc, for in 1760 he had offered a prize to the guides of Chamonix for the discovery of a practicable route to the summit. His intention was to repeat the ascent, once it had been made, and to achieve fame as the man who had made scientific observations on the highest point in the Alps.

The first serious attempt to climb Mont Blanc, and by far the most remarkable of all those which preceded the first ascent, was that of Jean-Nicolas Couteran, son of an innkeeper, and three guides, François and Michel Paccard, cousins of Dr Michel-Gabriel Paccard, and Victor Tissai, *dit le Chamois*. On July 14, 1775, this party actually reached the summit of the Dôme du Goûter (4,303 m., 14,120 feet) which is only 504 m., 1,653 feet lower than Mont Blanc (4,807 m., 15,771 feet).

The early history of Mont Blanc, of the first ascent and of the controversies which that first ascent provoked, is the subject of *The First Ascent of Mont Blanc,* a book which was selected by the Alpine Club to mark their centenary, and which fully deserved this honour. It is a model of Alpine scholarship. The book, published by the Oxford University Press, is the joint work of Professor Graham Brown, FRS, and Sir Gavin de Beer, FRS. Professor Graham Brown is a famous mountaineer, the pioneer of four superb routes on the Brenva face of Mont Blanc. Sir Gavin de Beer was elected to the Alpine Club on a literary qualification.

His *Travellers in the Alps* is an established classic. Both authors are distinguished scientists and thus possess the necessary quali-fications to pass judgment on de Saussure not only as a moun-taineer but also as a scientist.

### Paccard and Mont Blanc

Dr Michel-Gabriel Paccard (1757-1827) studied medicine at Turin, which was then the capital of the Kingdom of Sardinia, of which the Duchy of Savoy was a part, a fact which has led some Italians to claim that the first ascent of Mont Blanc was made by an Italian. Savoy was ceded to France as compensation for French support in the Italian war of liberation.

After post-graduate studies in Paris, at a time when Bourrit was also there, Paccard settled down in Chamonix as a doctor. In 1784 Paccard explored the approaches to Mont Blanc from the Glacier du Tacul and in the same year he made the first serious attempt on Mont Blanc by the Aiguille du Goûter, and stopped about 424 feet below the summit of the Aiguille. This was the first attempt to open the St Gervais route to Mont Blanc.

In 1785, Bourrit published a book in which he allegedly re-cords all the attempts which had been made till then to climb Mont Blanc, but in which he completely ignored Paccard's pioneer attempt by the St Gervais route which Bourrit claimed to have discovered. The second volume of de Saussure's *Voyages dans les Alpes* was published in April or May 1796. Paccard is nowhere mentioned in the book, and the whole credit for the dis-covery of the route via the Aiguille du Goûter is given to Bourrit.

Meanwhile, Dr Paccard had been examining Mont Blanc again and again through a telescope from the Brévent and other heights, and had decided to try his own route via the Grand Plateau and the Ancien Passage. He did not disclose his plans to Balmat, and Balmat's subsequent claim to have discovered the route is refuted by the fact that he told a shopkeeper to look out for them next day on the slopes of the Dôme du Goûter, obviously in the mistaken belief that Paccard intended to follow the tradi-tional line for attempts from the Montagne de la Côte.

Jacques Balmat had offered his services and was engaged not as a guide but as a porter. On August 7th, they bivouacked on the Montagne de la Côte, and left their bivouac at 4.15 next morning. At about 5 a.m. they entered the difficult ice labyrinth of the Jonction. On no less than four occasions members of the party broke through the small concealed crevasses and saved themselves by flinging themselves forward with poles horizontal to the snow. They had no rope. At some point above the Grands Mulets, Balmat felt that he had had enough. He told Paccard that his child was ill, and that he had promised to return to help his wife. Paccard dismissed the story of the sick child as a mere excuse, though in fact the child was ill and had died before they returned to Chamonix.

'If Dr Paccard had known about the child's serious illness, the attempt on Mont Blanc would necessarily have been postponed . . . his [Paccard's] own guide might return before another attempt could be made, and Balmat would be out of it . . . this must have been the reason for the callous concealment of the child's illness. It is difficult to see any other.'[1]

There was a second crisis when they reached the Grand Plateau. Once again Balmat refused to continue. They had been climbing for nine hours. The wind had risen, the temperature had fallen, and there was no certainty that they would reach the summit before sunset. Paccard's decision to continue was outstandingly courageous. We can understand Balmat's misgivings, and must give him full credit for overcoming his natural reluctance to continue. The Ancien Passage is steep. They reached the top at 5 p.m. They were observed from the valley to leave the Petits Mulets rocks at 6.12 p.m. and to reach the summit at 6.23 p.m. on August 8, 1786.

'What, however, is remarkable is that, after all they had gone through this day, the two of them climbed the final 384 feet of Mont Blanc in 11 minutes only—a rate of scarcely less than 2,100 feet an hour.'[2]

Paccard made a few observations, and after failing to find a rock suitable for a bivouac, they left the summit at 6.57 p.m. and reached the Montagne de la Côte before midnight.

[1] *The First Ascent of Mont Blanc*, p. 35. The second chapter contains a brilliant analysis of the first ascent, based on all available evidence.
[2] *Op. cit.*, p. 40.

Within a few hours of his return, Dr Paccard had told his story to Baron Adolf von Gersdorf who had followed the climb through his telescope. Von Gersdorf was 'well grounded in the natural sciences, was an excellent draughtsman, a keen topographer, a careful observer and a tireless diarist'. He had watched the climbers through an excellent achromatic telescope, and recorded what he saw 'with the fidelity of an unbiased observer and a responsible man of science'.[1]

Two months after the first ascent, Balmat signed an affidavit, duly witnessed by responsible citizens. In this important document, the French original of which is reproduced on page 419 of *The First Ascent of Mont Blanc*, Balmat provided all the necessary dynamite to destroy the Bourrit legend. He states (italics mine):

(1) that, knowing Paccard's guide to be away, he *volunteered* to accompany him;
(2) that success would have been impossible but for the 'regular pace' ('*marche régulière*') which Paccard maintained;
(3) that Paccard never ceased encouraging him, took some of the load which he had given Balmat to carry;
(4) that Paccard said that Balmat's desire to return to his wife was just an excuse;
(5) that Paccard showed him the way by his *new route*, and took the lead up a steep slope (the lower Ancien Passage);
(6) that Paccard led to the summit. '*He called me, I followed.*'
(7) that 'He fed me, he paid me, and handed to me the money which had been given to him for me' (presumably the prize which de Saussure had offered).

### The Birth of a Legend

In the first half of September Dr Paccard circulated a prospectus of a book describing the first ascent of Mont Blanc. The authors of *The First Ascent of Mont Blanc*, hereinafter referred to as 'the authors', suggested that what alarmed and angered Bourrit was the promise to include in this book a brief account of the previous attempts to climb Mont Blanc. Bourrit had claimed to have discovered the Aiguille du Goûter route, and had completely suppressed the fact that Paccard's all but successful attempt on

[1] *Op. cit.*, p. 156.

71

the Aiguille du Goûter had been made only a few days before Bourrit's attempt. It was therefore not only vanity but fear which prompted Bourrit in his attack on Paccard, an attack which succeeded in its disgraceful objective, for Paccard failed to get sufficient subscriptions for the publication of his book.

On September 20th, after the appearance of Dr Paccard's prospectus, Bourrit visited Chamonix, and it is a reasonable deduction from his subsequent actions that he saw Balmat and that he did his best to collect evidence which would injure Paccard.

On his return to Geneva, Bourrit issued his notorious pamphlet, dated September 20, 1786, which begins with a vainglorious account of his own attempts, and then proceeds to attack Paccard. He gives Balmat the sole credit for the discovery of the route, and for leadership on the mountain. He states that Paccard collapsed, that Balmat reached the summit alone and had to return to assist Paccard to the summit. De Saussure, on receipt of the pamphlet, seems to have protested in a letter which was lost but the contents of which can be deduced from Bourrit's reply. Unfortunately, that was de Saussure's one and only attempt to do justice to Paccard.

In the second issue of Bourrit's pamphlet (October 19, 1786), he added a postscript which did nothing to repair the damage to Paccard but which seems to have satisfied de Saussure who wrote, 'The postscript which you have added will put a little balm on the wound which the body of the Pamphlet cannot fail to inflict on the Doctor.' It was in the power of de Saussure completely to heal that wound, but he preferred, like the Levite in the parable of the Good Samaritan, to pass by on the other side. Paccard had fallen among thieves of his reputation, and he was long dead when the first of the good Samaritans appeared on the scene.

The Bourrit legend was perpetuated by Alexander Dumas who visited Chamonix in 1832 and interviewed Balmat. The lively and mendacious story which resulted was reprinted in many editions and translated into many languages.

The authors of *The First Ascent of Mont Blanc* apportion blame very justly between Bourrit and de Saussure. They write:

'One man, Professor de Saussure, could have killed the myth at its very beginning, and should have done so. The obvious venom in the *Pamphlet* itself, and in Bourrit's three letters to him, showed where the motive lay, and should have made the Professor distrust Bourrit's story—so different from what he himself learned from Balmat and Dr Paccard. It would have been easy for him to find out the truth of what had actually been seen during the ascent by writing to his friends, the innkeepers Couteran and Tairraz at Chamonix, and especially to von Gersdorf. Professor de Saussure had become involved in the events by his correspondence with Bourrit, and as an impartial man of science, it was his duty to ascertain the truth, and to defend it actively. Perhaps he had let his jealousy of Dr Paccard override his conscience, or political expedience frame his relations with Bourrit, but whatever may have been the factors which moved him, it is not easy to forgive the way in which he finally condoned Bourrit's attack so that he may almost be said to have supported it.'[1]

The authors give examples of de Saussure's intolerant attacks on men of science. 'His attack on Jean-André de Luc's hygrometry was regarded even by his own contemporaries as excessive, and his scathing remarks on Count Grégoire de Razoumowsky's mineralogical work were unnecessarily harsh.'

As scientists the authors are inevitably disturbed by de Saussure's deviations from the code which they rightly regard as binding on scientists, and not only on scientists. Phrases such as 'an impartial man of science' or 'as a man of science he had a conscience' are tolerant of an interpretation which the authors would certainly disclaim. One need not be a man of science to have a conscience and, at times, a guilty conscience, and there is no foundation for the theory that scientists, *as such*, are more impartial than other people where their own achievements and their own discoveries are concerned. Huxley, the great Victorian scientist, insisted that 'Science is no purer than any other sphere of human activity' and it was Huxley who described 'jealousy and pedantry' as 'the besetting sins' of scientists. A verdict which seems to me unnecessarily harsh. The man who is naturally generous will remain generous whatever profession he adopts, and the mean and envious will not be transferred into models of magnanimity by any training, scientific or humanistic.

[1] *Op. cit.*, p. 208.

*The Vindication of Dr Paccard*

Whymper in his *Guide to Chamonix* (1896) translated Balmat's affidavit, but was still too much under the influence of the Bourrit legend to do full justice to Paccard. The first serious challenge to the Balmat legend is to be found in C. E. Mathews's *The Annals of Mont Blanc*. Douglas Freshfield, inspired by Mathews's book, also made a useful contribution in an article contributed to the *Alpine Journal* (February 1899). A distinguished Swiss mountaineer, H. F. Montagnier, discovered Paccard's prospectus, the very existence of which had been questioned, and much new material in a bound volume of von Gersdorf's correspondence. Dr Dübi published this evidence in his important book, *Paccard wider Balmat* (1913). It was also Montagnier who found among the papers in the possession of de Saussure's grandson, the account of his interview with Paccard, which Freshfield translated and published in his *Life of de Saussure*, a book which leaves nothing intact of the Bourrit legend, but which is open to the serious objection that Freshfield does not allow the reader to suspect the sorry role played by de Saussure in this affair. The case against Balmat was admirably summarized by Mr E. H. Stevens in the *Alpine Journal* for May 1929, and finally Sir Gavin de Beer, 'after a long and seemingly hopeless search', discovered a document written by Dr Paccard himself during the climb, which recorded the barometric observations made during the ascent. This document provided the 'basic framework' for the admirable account of the climb in *The First Ascent of Mont Blanc*, a book which is not only perhaps the most outstanding contribution to Alpine scholarship in all the literature of mountaineering, but which is also as absorbing as a good detective story. The devastating effectiveness with which the case against Balmat and Bourrit is presented owes much to the skill with which slight clues are followed up, such as, for instance, the clues that can be deduced from the 'three decisive words' in Balmat's narratives of his various attempts and final ascent of Mont Blanc.

This book was, as I have said, officially chosen by the Alpine Club to mark their centenary year, a choice which is to be commended not only because the book fully merited this signal compliment but also for a less obvious reason. Let me explain.

Mountaineering in this century has been infected by national and ideological rivalries. Dictators have exploited mountaineer-

74

ing achievements in the interests of their respective ideologies, and are continuing so to do, as, for instance, in the grotesque claim of the Chinese Communists to have made the first ascent of Everest from Tibet, (a) after their oxygen had run out, (b) at night, and (c) at a time when, as we know from the leader of the Indian expedition on the other slope, a fierce storm was raging.

There is a disconcerting parallel between Bourrit's attempts to belittle Paccard and the hysterical campaign by extreme Indian nationalists to belittle Hillary's share in the first ascent of Everest. Balmat was engaged as a porter, and Tenzing, who was expert neither on ice nor on rock but was a superb leader of the Sherpa porters, was chosen by Sir John Hunt in generous recognition of all that the Sherpas had contributed to the Everest adventure. Nobody but a leader who refused to think in terms of national or racial rivalries, would have given a New Zealander and an Indian the chance to make the first ascent of Everest without an Englishman in the party. 'Reading the long accepted myth' (of Balmat's leading role), writes Sir John Hunt in his foreword to *The First Ascent of Mont Blanc*, 'I was reminded of the illustrations of an unconscious Hillary being dragged, hand over hand by the rope, to the summit of Everest by conquering Tenzing (who had no such notion) which adorned the triumphal arches along the road to Katmandu four years ago.'

Sir John Hunt was president of the Alpine Club when *The First Ascent of Mont Blanc* was selected as the centenary book. It would not have been unreasonable had the Club commissioned a history of the Alpine Club to mark the centenary. It is improbable that *The First Ascent of Mont Blanc* was consciously chosen to emphasize the tradition that national and ideological rivalries must not be allowed to infect the mountain brotherhood, but the fact that the Alpine Club celebrated its centenary by giving official patronage to a book describing a first ascent by a party which did not include a single British climber, and which took place more than half a century before the Alpine Club was founded, is convincing, if unintended, evidence of a serene indifference to the possibilities of exploiting this centenary for national propaganda.

## De Saussure's Alpine career

When de Saussure heard that Mont Blanc had been climbed, he

began to make preparations for his own ascent, and indeed hoped to climb Mont Blanc in the same summer, but it was not until the following year, 1787, that he succeeded. His climb received such immense publicity that not only Paccard but also Balmat was in danger of being forgotten, and de Saussure accepted as the first to climb Mont Blanc. I have, for instance, found in a book published as late as 1920, *Deux Peintres Suisses* by Conrad de Mandach, the statement (p. 14) that de Saussure made the first ascent of Mont Blanc.

In 1788 de Saussure spent sixteen days making scientific observations on the Col du Géant, an adventurous expedition which attracted a great deal of attention, and which was the subject of coloured prints signed 'Mechel', one of the Kleinmeisters of Switzerland. The Basle publisher must have believed that his prints would sell better if announced as illustrating de Saussure's ascent of Mont Blanc, and this deception was so successful that it has often been repeated as, for instance, in Bettex and Guillon's *Les Alpes Suisses dans la Littérature et dans l'Art* (p. 291).

None of de Saussure's contemporaries or predecessors had travelled more extensively in the Alps. Of the easy passes which he crossed, many of them several times, may be mentioned the Grimsel, Furka, Gries, Splügen, Great Scheidegg and the passes traversed on the tour of Monte Rosa and on the tour of Mont Blanc. From Engelberg he climbed a minor summit above the Joch Pass, and from Courmayeur the Cramont. His glacier expeditions include Mont Blanc, the Col du Géant, the little Mont Cervin, the Théodule Pass and the Zäsenberg above Grindelwald.

And yet, de Saussure's main motive was neither exploration nor mountaineering but scientific and, in particular, geological research. 'What was wanting in de Saussure,' writes Freshfield, 'was the element of rashness that makes a pioneer. It was Bourrit's example that urged him to his first serious attempts and failure on Mont Blanc. It was the success of Paccard and Balmat that spurred him to follow them. It was Exchaquet who induced him to camp on the Col du Géant. He preferred the comparative certainty of reaching a goal already proved attainable to the zest of a new and doubtful adventure. It was in this respect that he differed from the average modern mountaineer to whom the climb itself is the main object, and the exertion its own reward.'[1]

[1] *Op. cit.,* p. 285.

De Saussure's mountain journeys are described in the four volumes of his *Voyages dans les Alpes*, which were published volume by volume at Neuchâtel (1779, 1786, 1790, 1796). That the *Voyages* stimulated interest in mountains is certain, but his writings could hardly awaken in the reader emotions which he himself had not felt. He makes no comment on one of the loveliest Alpine views, the Jungfrau from the Wengernalp, or on the Wetterhorn from Rosenlaui, that favourite theme of the early mountain artists from Lory to Calame, and one bald sentence suffices to record his impression of the Matterhorn.

Only some strong stimulus to his imagination, such as a mountain bivouac beneath the stars, could evoke from de Saussure an expression of awe in the presence of the mountains. And it is significant that the most striking tribute to mountain scenery in his writings is a description of the mountains when their authentic beauty was *concealed* by darkness. It was the mystery and awe of the mountains at night, not their beauty, which inspired his description of a night on the Tête Rousse. Here is the passage in question:

'Le ciel était parfaitement pur et sans nuages; la vapeur ne se voyait plus que dans le fond des vallées: brillantes, mais dépouillées de toute espèce de scintillations, repandaient sur les sommités des montagnes une lueur extrêment faible et pâle, mais qui suffisait pourtant à faire distinguer les masses et les distances. Le repos et le profond silence qui régnaient dans cette vaste étendue, agrandi encore par l'imagination, m'inspiraient une sorte de terreur; il me semblait que j'avais survécu à l'universe, et que je voyais son cadavre étendu sous mes pieds.'

### De Saussure's Last Years

De Saussure rendered great services to Geneva during the difficult years of political strife and revolution. The concessions which the Patricians were prepared to make to the disfranchised *natifs* proved to be both too little and too late. The result was the revolution of April 1782 in which there was street fighting and bloodshed. De Saussure himself withstood a six-day siege in his home.

De Saussure hoped to save the State by the formation of a middle party of moderates. That he was certainly not a reactionary was proved by the enthusiasm with which he welcomed the

French Revolution. He was at Macugnaga when the Bastille fell, and he records his delight in a diary entry for July 27th.

'My letters bring very good news from home, and of the happy revolution at Paris and Versailles. This brings balm to my soul.'

Like other intellectuals, de Saussure was a victim of that recurring illusion that the overthrow of a corrupt government will mean the end of corruption. 'Individuals and masses,' to quote Burckhardt, 'attribute everything that irks them to the existing dispensation while for the most part what they are suffering under is inherent in human nature.'

It was soon apparent that the 'Egaliseurs' of Geneva were ambitious to rival the rabble of Paris—'apes imitating tigers', as Madame de Staël called them. On July 24, 1794, the apes produced an imitation of the tigers by the terrible Massacre on the Bastions. Many of the patrician families left Geneva during the crisis, but de Saussure remained at his post, determined to do all that was possible to act as a check on the 'apes'. And it is certain that but for his moderating influence the excesses would have been far worse.

The Revolution which, as we have seen, brought balm to de Saussure's soul, also brought the armies of revolutionary France into Switzerland. On April 15, 1798, the independence of Geneva ended for ever, for when Napoleon had been defeated, Geneva was incorporated in the Swiss Confederation. De Saussure, who had invested most of his money in France, would have been reduced to poverty but for the fact that his wife had invested her fortune with greater prudence. On the morning of January 22, 1799, de Saussure died in the arms of his son, Theodore. He was buried on January 24th. The professors and students of the Academy and the representatives of the Societies of Arts and Natural History followed the coffin to the cemetery of Plainplace and laid the great Genevese to rest in a grave, the position of which it is now impossible to ascertain.

# 8

## 'PERHAPS THE FIRST OF THE
## TRUE MOUNTAINEERS'

IN HIS interesting introduction to the 'Lonsdale Library' volume on *Mountaineering*, Professor T. Graham Brown, FRS, describes Father Placidus a Specha as 'perhaps the first of the true mountaineers', a view with which I agree. Father Placidus was remarkable not only as a mountaineer but also as a scholar and scientist. A brief outline of his stormy career is desirable before considering his mountaineering achievements.

Father Placidus was by birth a citizen of the republic of the Grisons, the Canton which includes St Moritz, Davos and the Bündner Oberland, Father Placidus's native region. It was not until Napoleon had been finally crushed that the Grisons became a member of the Swiss Confederation. Until then it had been, like the Valais, Neuchâtel and Geneva, an Allied State.

Father Placidus was born on December 9, 1752, in the little village of Truns, in the valley which begins at the Oberalp pass, separating the Canton of Uri from the Canton of the Grisons. This valley is part of the region known as the Bündner Oberland which, unlike most of the Canton of the Grisons, is predominantly Catholic.

Father Placidus was the son of peasants, and as a boy spent many weeks every year looking after his flocks and herds. His first great interest was his collection of crystals, in the search for which he laid the foundation of his mountaineering experience. His mother attributed his skill on rocks to the fact that he was born when the sun was in Capricorn. His parents, who must have recognized clear evidence of talent, sent him to school at the age of ten, where he learned to write Romansch, his native tongue, and to read German. Three years later he entered the seminary at Chur. Among the subjects which he studied at Chur was music. In many of the trials of his later life he found great consolation in his violin.

In 1774 he entered the Benedictine Abbey of Disentis. Two years later he was transferred for a few years to the great Benedictine Abbey of Einsiedeln. At that time the Abbot was a great scholar and, in part at least, responsible for the atmosphere of intellectual activity which Father Placidus found at Einsiedeln, and which had such a stimulating effect on him. He delighted in the excellent library, but was unimpressed by the collection of crystals and promised that on his return to Disentis he would select some crystals from his own collection and present them to Einsiedeln.

In 1782 Father Placidus returned to Disentis, and in the same year was transferred to the Hospital St Johann on the Lukmanier pass just above Disentis, where he spent the next seven years. It was on the Lukmanier that his career as a mountain explorer began. During those years he devoted such time as he could spare to exploring and climbing the surrounding heights, and to collecting crystals. Many of his observations were committed to paper, and gradually he became known outside his native valley. Almost all those who visited Disentis in the course of their studies sought him out and asked for his advice. In 1790, he initiated what was to prove a long and fruitful correspondence with the Bernese scientist Samuel Wyttenbach. It was also during this period that Father Placidus began his studies of his own native language, Romansch, which is now one of the four official languages of Switzerland.

These years of mountain exploration and scholarly research came to an abrupt end when the armies of revolutionary France invaded Switzerland. Father Placidus had made no secret of his sympathy with many of the new ideas which were being proclaimed by the French, and this naturally brought him into sharp opposition not only to the clergy but also to the local population. He was attacked as a godless Jacobin, and denounced to the Austrians as a partisan of the French. When the Austrians entered Disentis, Father Placidus was forced to hand over to the Austrian Captain Schöllheim some of his writings and maps. He particularly regretted the loss of a map of Medels, Tavetsch and Disentis on which he had laboured for a whole year.

Meanwhile detachments of the French army had reached the Oberalp pass and were advancing rapidly down the valley towards Disentis. The Abbot and most of the monks fled, but Father

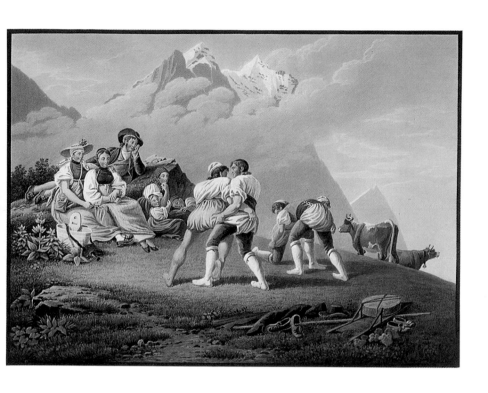

12  GABRIEL LORY, FILS (1784–1846). Wrestlers in the Bernese Oberland. In
the background Wellhorn, Wetterhorn and Eiger. Coloured copper engraving

Placidus refused to leave the Abbey, and after the defeat of the Austrians near Disentis on March 7, 1799, he arranged for the French wounded to be transported to the best room in the Abbey. The monks tended the wounded, and earned the temporary gratitude of the French, but before long the pattern of expropriation reappeared. Everything of value in the Abbey, including Father Placidus's collections of crystals, was removed to Chur. A contribution of 100,000 gold livres had been demanded from the Abbey. Father Placidus on his own initiative approached the French Adjutant-General, and persuaded him to reduce his demands by 20,000 livres, a success which his clerical enemies exploited as evidence of his sympathy with the hated Jacobins.

During a second visit to Chur, Father Placidus heard that the population in the Bündner Oberland had risen against the French, news which filled him with dismay, for he realized all too clearly that they had no hope of success. The members of the Provisional Government in Chur and the Helvetic Commissars begged Father Placidus to establish contact with the leaders of the revolt and to offer them immunity if they laid down their arms. He failed in his mission, and the revolt, as he had foreseen, was crushed. Father Placidus hurried back to Disentis only to find the Abbey a smoking ruin, his own precious manuscripts and notes having perished in the flames. As the only monk in Disentis, he took up his residence in a peasant's house, and took charge of the Abbey's interests.

The French did not long remain masters of the Bünder Oberland. On May 14th they were defeated and forced to evacuate the valley, which was speedily occupied by the Austrians. Whereupon Father Placidus's heroic interventions with the French in the interests of the Abbey turned against him. He was summoned to Chur, accused by the Austrians of handing over to the French the maps and notes that he had compiled on his mountain wanderings, and further charged with failing to instil in the population due reverence for the House of Austria and hatred of the French. He replied that the first charge was false, and the second did not concern him. 'Als Bürger einer Freyen Republik stehe es mir frey ind uneingeschränkt zu denken, als Priester aber über Tugend und Laster nach der Answeisung des hohen Evangeliums zu reden.'[1]

---

[1] 'As the free citizen of a Republic' (the reference is not to the Swiss Con-

This courageous answer impressed his accusers, and he was released.

Shortly after his return to Disentis he preached a sermon on the text '*Nolite confidere in principibus, in filibus hominum, in quibus non est salus*' : 'Put not your trust in princes nor in the sons of men in whom there is no help' (Psalm 146), and urged his congregation to put their trust in God and in the intercession of the Saints rather than in the rulers of this world, but his enemies delated him for attempting to evoke distrust of the Imperial Austrian authority. He was arrested and transported to Innsbruck on September 6, 1799, and lodged in the Servite monastery, where he remained until February 23, 1801. The community did all in their power to render his enforced stay agreeable, and the civil authorities soon relaxed any restrictions on his movements. Among his published works are a description of a journey from Innsbruck to Schwatz in Tirol and a journey to the Patscher Kofel in August 1800. He became so attached to Innsbruck that he might have remained indefinitely but for his longing to return to his native land.

On his return to Disentis his relations with the Abbot were never satisfactory, and after various vicissitudes, described in detail by Professor Pieth of Chur in the monumental biography,[1] Father Placidus returned in 1817 as parish priest to his birthplace, Truns, and it was there that he died in his eighty-second year on August 14, 1833. According to tradition his last words, in his native Romansch, were '*Ussa dat la baracca ensemen*' : 'Now the barracks are collapsing.'

Mr Francis Gribble devoted a chapter to Father Placidus in his book *The Early Mountaineers*. Mr Gribble specialized in the romances of the great, and his books, *Madame de Staël and Her Lovers, Georges Sand and Her Lovers, Rousseau and the Women he Loved, Chateaubriand and His Court of Women*, were the products of patient and scholarly research; but the love of God was not his subject, and his knowledge of Benedictine monasti-

federation, which did not at that time include the canton of the Grisons, but to the independent Republic of Grisons) 'I am free to think as I will, and as a priest to speak of virtue and vice in accordance with the teaching of the Holy Gospel.'
[1] *Pater Placidus a Spescha.* Herausgegeben von Prof. Dr Fried. Pieth, Chur und Prof. Dr P. Karl Hager, Disentis. Verlag Benteli, Bümpliz-Bern 1913.

cism may be deduced from the fact that he refers to Father Placidus as a Friar.

As Gribble could not understand how a man as intelligent as Father Placidus could possibly wish to enter a monastery, he introduces his guesses by such phrases as 'in all probability' and 'one can imagine'. Yes, one can always—imagine.

'One can imagine that it was largely for the purpose of escaping from the uncongenial company of his fellow friars [sic] that Father Placidus, at this period of his life, resumed the practice of mountaineering. It may also have been that the controversial trivialities with which they troubled him seemed more trivial than ever upon the hill-tops, and that he repaired to the hill-tops with the deliberate aim of enjoying the sense of their insignificance.'

Gribble, of course, assumed that an intelligent monk who had trouble with his ecclesiastical superiors was necessarily the victim of clerical bigotry, and consequently Gribble's Father Placidus conforms closely to the convention of rationalist folklore. Father Placidus was, however, anything but an innocent and uncomplaining victim, for on balance he gave as good as he got. One can admire his courage and his independence, and yet realize that he must often have maddened his fellow-countrymen, both lay and clerical, particularly in his attitude to the French Revolution.

'At first,' he wrote, 'I gave my adherence to the Republic and demanded that there should be more freedom in the land, and that everybody should be free fearlessly to express his views.'

Father Placidus made no secret of his sympathy with the French Revolutionaries. 'Because freedom was near to my heart,' he wrote, 'I inclined to the French party.'

Father Placidus sympathized with the French because he believed that they at least wished to extend the boundaries of freedom, whereas he suspected the Austrians of plans to annex the Grisons. 'Every revolution,' as the great Basel historian Burckhardt remarks, 'opens with the brilliant farce of hope.' In England, most intellectuals sympathized at the outset with the French Revolution, just as in our time most intellectuals began by sympathizing with the Bolshevik Revolution, but the invasion of Switzerland by the armies of revolutionary France profoundly shocked many whose faith in the Revolution had been eroded but not wholly destroyed by the Terror. The attack upon Switzerland by a power claiming to be in the vanguard of progress produced much the same effect as the attack on democratic Finland by Soviet Russia in 1939. Wordsworth wrote the famous sonnet (*Thoughts of a Briton on the subjugation of Switzerland*) which begins:

> 'Two Voices are there; one is of the sea,
> One of the mountains; each a mighty voice:
> In both from age to age thou didst rejoice,
> They were thy chosen music, Liberty!'

The French not only ruthlessly plundered the country which they claimed to have liberated—even the bears from the bear-pit in Berne were sent to Paris—but they imposed on Switzerland a despotism incomparably more irksome than that of the Habsburgs against which the Forest Cantons had revolted. 'The liberty of the Revolution' was, as Burckhardt remarked, 'the liberty of a forest fire, free to devour all that lay in the path of its flames.'

Father Placidus's hopes that the Grisons, by a policy of strict neutrality, might escape these horrors, were doomed to be disappointed. The country folk in the Bünder Oberland hated the French not only because they had invaded Switzerland, but also because the Revolutionary Government had enthroned a prostitute in Notre Dame, and repudiated the Catholic religion. Father Placidus's position, as a sympathizer with the Jacobins in a predominantly Catholic population, might be compared to the position of the 'Red' Dean of Canterbury in England.

'The ideas of that period,' writes Dr Pieth, 'found in this enlightened man an enthusiastic supporter. He made no secret of his views, and thus found himself in the harshest political opposition to the ecclesiastics and the great majority of his fellow-countrymen.'

It was not only Father Placidus's political views which shocked the Catholics, but also his views on clerical celibacy. In the course of his historical researches he had discovered that a parish priest who had worked in the Bünder Oberland towards the end of the fifteenth century had been married, a discovery which prompted him to write a pamphlet in which he maintained that celibacy had been illegally introduced into the Western Church.[1]

There was, of course, nothing heretical in such views, for the celibacy of the clergy, though part of the discipline, is not part of the defined doctrine of the Catholic Church. Indeed, there are Uniate Churches, such as the Maronites, in full communion with Rome, in which priests are allowed to marry. But this attack on clerical celibacy was not calculated to endear him to his superiors. In the written record of his mountain wanderings, he records the fact that the parish priest of Campo, with whom he spent a night, attributed the shortage of priests in the valley to the celibacy of the clergy. One wonders whether Father Placidus was discreet enough to keep this conversation to himself, or did he take an early opportunity to quote the parish priest to those of his fellow monks who were well aware of his views on celibacy? And celibacy was not the only point on which his views were eccentric. In a discussion during a chapter meeting, Father Placidus decisively repudiated as terroristic the traditional teaching that the member of a religious Order owed unconditional obedience to his Superior.

It was, perhaps, because he found the vow of obedience difficult to keep that he applied to his Bishop for permission to enter the ranks of the secular clergy. At first this request was refused, but it is clear that the Abbot was prepared to give him permission to leave the Abbey and accept a post as parish priest provided that a suitable parish could be found. The Abbot appears to have made difficulties in the case of two of the benefices which Father Placidus coveted. In these particular cases he attempted to bring pressure by methods which his sympathetic biographer, Dr Pieth, could not approve. On the first of these occasions he tried to enlist the active support of the hated French usurpers in Berne, and on the second he even suggested to the Gemeinde at Brigels that they should threaten to withhold their annual tribute to the Abbey if the Abbot did not consent to his being appointed parish priest.

In 1817 the Abbot gave him permission to accept the post of parish priest in Truns, his birthplace, and he remained there until he died on August 14, 1833.

The ambivalent attitude of the Benedictines of Disentis to Father Placidus is understandable. They disapproved of many of

[1] *Widerrechtliche Einführung des Cölibats in der abendländischen Kirche.*

his views, but they had a great respect for his intellectual achievements and for his regional patriotism. They themselves were pro-Austrian because the Austrian Emperor was a defender of the Faith, whereas the French were the enemies of the Church, but they may well have condoned Father Placidus's antipathy to the Austrians because this was recognized to be an expression of his devotion to the language and to the Romansch way of life. They knew that the Romansch language had with difficulty survived the infiltration of German, and needed scholarly champions as patriotic as Father Placidus.

No religious Order has a greater respect for learning than the Benedictines, and Father Placidus's fellow Benedictines were certainly aware of his great contributions not only to the study and defence of the Romansch language but also to the history of the Abbey, which previous historians had covered only as far as 1705 and which Father Placidus had brought up to date. Finally, they knew that Father Placidus's fame as a naturalist and as a cartographer extended far beyond the confines of the Bünder Oberland. Dr Pieth, who writes with great admiration of Father Placidus and considerable sympathy of his difficulties with his ecclesiastical superiors, admits that he did not improve the situation by his obstinacy and stubbornness ('*dass Spescha durch seinen Eigensinn und Trotz die Situation nicht verbessert hat*').

Father Placidus was undoubtedly difficult as a member of a religious community and yet, in spite of his political views and in spite of his eccentric ideas, he seems, apart from one short period, to have been treated with great forbearance. He appears to have had no difficulty in obtaining permission for his mountain explorations, some of which lasted many days. The Abbot fell in with his views when he wished to leave the monastery. He enjoyed swimming against the ecclesiastical stream, and it is therefore ridiculous to write as if the inevitable reactions of more conventional ecclesiastics were either surprising or reprehensible. Whereas Gribble persuades himself that Father Placidus was a pathetic innocent monk persecuted by ecclesiastical bigots, I am impressed by the restraint of the Benedictines and by the clear evidence of their tolerance of Father Placidus's marked deviation from the Benedictine norm. The Benedictines must, I believe, have felt that though Father Placidus was excessively troublesome to his contemporaries, his achievements would be recalled with pride by later Benedictines, and if they argued thus, history was to vindicate both their prescience and their tolerance.

That Father Placidus was the first of the true mountaineers is a statement which it would be difficult to dispute. Gesner, who loved the mountains, and who returned to them again and again, only attempted easy expeditions such as Pilatus. He was not a mountaineer in the modern sense of the term. Though passes had been climbed from time immemorial, few rock and snow peaks had been climbed before Father Placidus's mountaineering career began. Of those whose mountaineering achievements I described in the last chapter, de Saussure alone may be said to have made a regular practice of climbing, but his climbs were all concentrated into a period of only a few years (1776-1792) and his main, perhaps his only, motive appears to have been scientific. Father Placidus, though keenly interested in the scientific aspects of his mountain wanderings, loved the mountains for their own sake and anticipated in many of his reactions not only to mountains but to mountaineering, the attitude of the founding fathers of the Alpine Club.

Father Placidus lost many of the records of his earlier climbs in the Disentis fire, but the incomplete list of his ascents on pages 461-463 of the Pieth-Hager biography contains records of mountain expeditions in no less than twenty-five seasons, the first of which was in 1782. In that year he climbed the Piz Crystallina (10,266 feet) in the Medelsertal and the Scopi (10,500 feet) above the Lukmanier. Among his many first ascents may be mentioned the Stockgron (11,214 feet), near and only a little lower than the Tödi, in 1782; the Rheinwaldhorn (11,175 feet), the highest peak overlooking the sources of the Rhine, probably in 1789; the Güferhorn (11,142 feet), the second highest peak of the Rheinwaldhorn group, in 1806; the Oberalpstock (10,926 feet), the highest point in the immediate neighbourhood of Disentis, probably in 1793; and the Piz Urlaun (11,060 feet), near the Tödi, in 1793.

In the ranges north of the Rheinwaldhorn, Father Placidus made the following first ascents: the Piz Aul (10,250 feet) in 1792, the Piz Terri (10,338 feet) in 1801 or 1802; and the Piz Scharboden (10,250 feet), date unknown.

The records of his climbs between 1793 and 1799 are lost, but it is more than probable that he continued to climb during these years.

In his description of a mountaineering expedition in 1823 he writes:

'From my youth onwards I was interested in the study of nature and of geography, and found in the mountains everything which could satisfy my tastes. I was ambitious to preserve my health and to strengthen my body; as a result of my efforts in mountains and valleys I have kept my health for forty years and am still strong and cheerful.'[1]

No other mountaineer of the period had a record comparable to that of Father Placidus. His mountaineering career attained its apotheosis on the first ascent of the Tödi (11,887 feet). True, Father Placidus himself did not reach the summit, but he climbed high enough to have, in his own words, many glaciers under his feet.

In his seventy-third year this gallant veteran reached a gap only 863 feet below the summit, a gap which is now known as the Porta da Spescha. From this point he watched his companions, the chamois-hunter Placidus Curschellas of Truns and Augustin Bisquolm of Disentis, reach the actual summit.

A wonderful climax to a wonderful mountaineering career.

Father Placidus made a definite contribution to mountain knowledge, not only by the record of his ascents but also by the book that he published in 1800 containing practical advice to mountaineers, and by his maps. The three-pronged crampons which he attached to the heels of his boots have been preserved. In some of his climbs he used both rope and ice-axe.

He writes with unjustifiable contempt of the barometer as an aid to map-making, and it is amazing what good maps he produced considering that he only made use of primitive instruments which he had made himself. Of his map, *Carte spécielle et pétrographique du Mont St-Gothard et de ces environs*, Professor J. Königsberger, a distinguished geologist, wrote in 1903, 'this map could still be used' (*'Diese Karte ist heute noch brauchbar'*). If Father Placidus's interest in the mountains had been only

[1] Pieth u. Hager, *op. cit.*, page lxxxiii.

13  HORACE-BÉNÉDICT DE SAUSSURE (1740–1799), mountaineer and explorer.
Contemporary coloured copper engraving

14   PATER PLACIDUS A SPESCHA (1752–1833), mountaineer. Contemporary
woodcut

15  LUDWIG VOGEL (1788–1879). Drawing Engelberg 1825. (Schweiz. Landes-
museum Zürich)

16 MATTERHORN GLACIER. Lithography by H. Nicolet from Louis Agassiz «Etudes sur les glaciers», Neuchâtel 1840

or mainly scientific, he would have no claim to be regarded as 'the first of the real mountaineers', for the real mountaineer loves the mountains for themselves, and enjoys mountaineering as a sport irrespective of any additions to his own scientific knowledge that he may acquire in the course of his expeditions.

It is always rash to dogmatize about motives, but my own tentative conclusion is that Agassiz, the father of the glacial-epoch theory, was not a real mountaineer. He spent weeks in the Unteraar glacier studying glacier motion, but the only big peak that he appears to have climbed was the Jungfrau. He spent the last years of his life in America, and never once returned to his native Switzerland. If there is any passage in his writings which could be interpreted as nostalgia for the Alps, I should be grateful to have my attention drawn to it. I do not pretend to have read every line he wrote, but I have certainly found nothing to suggest that Agassiz was interested in any but the scientific aspects of mountains in general and glaciers in particular.

Father Placidus climbed many mountains in the course of his map-making, but more often than not he left his primitive instruments behind, and his reaction to the all but unexplored mountain world reminds me of the ingenuous pleasure which the mountains evoked in the contributors to *Peaks, Passes and Glaciers*. Father Placidus's joy in summit panoramas is apparent in many passages, such as the description of a view, '*Die Aussicht war prachtvoll*' ('the view was glorious'). He continues: 'My pen cannot convey the enjoyment which was mine on this mountain peak. I could only wish that such wanderings could often be my lot.'[1] A wish which was destined to be gratified.

The true mountain lover will often repeat an ascent. The Scopi above Lukmanier was climbed three times by Father Placidus.

Father Placidus's happiness in the mere fact of being on a mountain top finds expression in many of his passages as, for instance, in his recollections of an hour spent on the summit of the Tschima. After contrasting the debased amusements of the plains with the simplicity of nature as revealed on the mountains, he adds: 'I left the Tschima as unwillingly as the disciples left

---

[1] '*Des frohen Genuss, den ich auf diesem Berggipfel empfand, kann meine Feder nicht entwerfen; ich wünschte nur, ich bekäme oft Gelegenheit, ähnliche Bergreisen auzustellen.*'

Mount Thabor after the transfiguration of Our Lord."[1] There speaks the voice of the authentic mountain lover.

Towards the end of his long life Father Placidus summed up the creed of the happy mountain warrior in words which seem to me to link him in apostolic succession to Gesner among his predecessors, and to Leslie Stephen and Geoffrey Winthrop Young among his successors:

'I am not surprised in my old age to be asked, after forty years of wanderings among the mountains and valleys of the Alps, exposed to heat, cold and storm, what conclusions I have drawn from those mountain travels and what advice I can offer. As I write these words I recall those mountain days with the greatest joy and satisfaction. Never, I am sure, were my days so full of feeling and of happiness.'

[1] *Man verlässt die Tschima so ungern, als die Jünger des Herrn nach seiner verklärung den Berg Thabor verlassen haben.'*

# 9

## LOUIS AGASSIZ

---

AGASSIZ was born on May 28, 1807, at Môtier on the shores of Lake Morat. Agassiz's father was a Protestant pastor who came of a family of which six generations had been ministers of religion, in direct descent from a Huguenot who had fled from France to Switzerland after the revocation of the Edict of Nantes. Louis Agassiz was the fifth child, but the eldest of those who survived, for the first four children had all died before Louis was born. He went to school at Bienne and Lausanne, and attended the universities of Zürich, Heidelberg and Munich. Louis was intended by his father for the medical profession, and he obediently took his medical degree, but he never wavered in his determination to become, as he told his father, 'the first naturalist of my time'.

At Munich he helped a fellow student, Karl von Martius, to classify a cargo of fishes which von Martius had brought back from the Amazon. This proved to be a turning point in his life, for he first became known as a leading authority on fishes both living and fossilized, and this at the early age of twenty-one.

His father reluctantly gave him permission to conclude his medical studies in Paris, and it was there, at the age of twenty-four, that he made the acquaintance of those great scientists, Cuvier and Humboldt. Cuvier, who was then very old, had abandoned his own ambition to write a book about fishes, and generously turned over his material to Agassiz. Alexander von Humboldt secured for him some paid work as a teacher, but for which his financial position would have been even more precarious than it was. Both Cuvier and Humboldt were inscribed on that long list of benefactors without whose help Agassiz would probably never have achieved world-wide fame.

Agassiz's career would have been far less distinguished but for the fact that he was born 'helpee', a word which is badly needed to distinguish between two antithetical types, the born *helpers* whose vocation it is to help other people, and the born *helpees* who have a genius for persuading other people to help them. The helpee would be far less successful if he could not, without conscious effort, convince helpers that in helping him they are rendering a great service, not to a mere individual but also to some great cause, religion or art or, as in the case of Agassiz, science. The most successful helpees are those who, like Agassiz himself, are completely disinterested. 'Certain sayings of Agassiz,' writes that great American philosopher, William James, 'as the famous one that he had "no time for making money", have caught the public fancy.' Public fancy, perhaps, but Frau Karl Marx's wistful complaint, 'If only Karl would make some capital instead of writing about it', would have evoked an immediate response from Agassiz's long-suffering wife.

Not only had Agassiz 'no time for making money', but he would have been uneasy had any money which he did make remained long enough in his pockets to be invested. He insisted that a man who exploited his knowledge to make money was unworthy of the name of savant. His only use for money was to spend it to advance scientific knowledge, and the money which he saved in America was given to the museum which he founded at Cambridge, Mass. At his death he had no real property other than his books and a house which was already mortgaged. He left the house to his wife and those of his scientific books which he might select from his father's library to his son, Alexander, on the condition that when he had no further use for them he would add them to the rest of Agassiz's books which he had already bequeathed to the Museum of Comparative Zoology. And yet Agassiz might easily have died a very rich man. The University of California had offered him a chair at an annual salary of 20,000 dollars, the equivalent then of 100,000 Swiss francs, or £4,000 a year. When we compare income tax and the value of money in 1870 with income tax and the value of money today, it is clear that Agassiz was rejecting the possibility of making a modest fortune. It was not only because Agassiz was completely disinterested that there was never a shortage of helpers at his disposal, but also because he had exceptional charm. Certainly his talent for enlisting unpaid help developed young. As he was an indifferent draughtsman, he was always in need of assistants to draw or sketch or paint his zoological specimens. At the age of ten, his little sister, Cécile, was already making sketches of the specimens which her brother had laboriously collected in the neighbourhood. At Munich, where his allowance was 1,300 Swiss francs a year, little more than the equivalent of £50 sterling,[1] he was already maintaining two artists in his employment to paint fishes.

'This may sound strange,' he wrote in a brief memoir dictated to his wife, 'for I only had 1,200-1,300 francs at my disposal. How then could I employ two artists? But they were as poor as I was, and accustomed as we were to live from very little, we managed to get along, sharing fraternally our modest resources.'[2]

From the age of twenty onwards he always had one or more artists, naturalists or secretaries in attendance, the usual arrangement being that they would be paid in so far as money was available, and if not, not. In November 1832 he took up an appointment at Neuchâtel to give 'auditoires' in various parts of the city. It was not until 1841 that the so-called Academy was founded or until 1909 that this Academy evolved into a university.

In 1832 there were only a hundred students, but before long his lecture rooms were crowded not only by students but by their elders. He was a remarkably successful teacher. One of his most famous pupils was Johann Jakob von Tschudi. We are indebted to Dr Paul Emil Schatzmann for a fascinating biography of von Tschudi published by the *Verlag Mensch und Arbeit* in Zürich. Tschudi spent five years exploring the Peruvian peaks as a naturalist, and the works which he published on his return established his reputation. After various diplomatic missions to the Court of Don Pedros in Brazil, he ended his career as Swiss Minister in Vienna. Throughout his life he continued to correspond with Agassiz.

Agassiz meanwhile had married a German lady, Cäcilie Braun,

---

[1] I am indebted to the distinguished economist, Dr Paul Einzig, for the information that £50 sterling in 1830 was the equivalent in purchasing value of £250 today.

[2] *On trouvera ceci peut-être étrange, car, moi qui n'avais que 12 à 1300 fr. par an à ma disposition, comment pouvais-je entretenir deux artistes? Mais ils étaient eux-mêmes bien plus pauvres que moi, et, habitués que nous étions à vivre de peu, nous trouvions moyen de cheminer ainsi en partageant fraternellement nos faibles ressources.'

the sister of Alexander Braun, who had been a close friend of Agassiz at Munich and who remained a close friend throughout his life. This did not, however, prevent Braun giving his sister excellent advice on the disadvantages of marrying a genius. Sound advice, for Cily, as her family called her, was never happy at Neuchâtel, and never ceased to regret her home in Karlsruhe. Louis was very fond of her, but science was his first and only mistress, and poor Cily had to adjust herself to the role of being merely one among many helpers. This was all the more trying because Agassiz's helpers were nothing but hindrances so far as she was concerned, hindrances to all hope of a normal married life with her erratic husband.

The first volume of Agassiz's *Recherches sur les poissons fossiles* was an immediate success. The book obtained for Agassiz the award of the Prix Cuvier and, what was more important, a welcome from the scientific élite when he paid his first visit to England. In the course of six weeks he saw all the more important scientific museums in England and Scotland and also many private collections. Darwin had already embarked on the sea voyage which was to have such momentous consequences, but Agassiz met and was entertained by Charles Lyell, Adam Sedgwick, the Earl of Enniskillen, and by Professor Buckland at Christ Church. Agassiz fell in love with England in general and with Oxford in particular.

Unpleasant surprises awaited Agassiz on his return to Neuchâtel. His monumental work on fish fossils, with his numerous and costly illustrations, a work of which only the first volume had been published, would have strained the resources of his publisher even if Agassiz had been less extravagant in his demands. Only the best was good enough for Agassiz, and the despairing publisher abandoned the book. 'There's nothing for it,' said Agassiz, 'but to become my own publisher. My only security is in success, and I am convinced that I shall carry this work through to a successful conclusion, even though at night I often don't know how I will carry on next day.' How, for instance, to meet the printing bill? His family, we are told, helped him with loans, 'at first with pleasure, afterwards with reluctance'. Humboldt also lent him money. 'I was pleased,' wrote Agassiz, 'to remain a debtor to Humboldt,' happy, that is, to feel that he had made it possible for Humboldt to be of service to—science.

Agassiz is remembered today far less for his classification of fishes than as the first scientist to popularize the theory of the great ice ages. His interest in glaciers began during a summer which he spent at the home of another great Swiss scientist, de Charpentier. Charpentier had married a charming German lady who was very kind to her compatriot, Madame Agassiz, a kindness which was all the more appreciated because Cily had never succeeded in making any real friends among the ladies of Neuchâtel. This summer with the Charpentiers was perhaps the happiest in Cily's married life.

While Cily explained to her hostess how difficult it was to be married to a genius, a subject on which, as we know, she felt strongly, Agassiz and Charpentier talked glaciers.

Glaciers in retreat leave behind 'erratic boulders', that is, boulders composed of rocks different from the rocks on which they lie, a granite boulder, for instance, resting on limestone. Terminal moraines, again, are often found many miles, in some cases many hundreds of miles, from the glaciers which deposited them. The evidence for the former extension of glaciers is indeed so obvious that it is difficult to understand the failure of eminent scientists such as de Saussure to appreciate the significance of terminal moraines which he saw on his travels, the terminal moraines, for instance, at Ivres, many miles from the glaciers which once extended far beyond Ivres into the plains of Italy. It seems that B. J. Kun, of whom little is known, was the first to suggest, in an essay published in 1787, that such ancient moraines were evidence of the former great extension of Alpine glaciers. In 1802 and in 1816 John Playfair was independently led to the same conclusions by the study of erratic boulders, but he made little attempt to convert the world to his beliefs. Meanwhile, a simple peasant and chamois hunter in the little village of Lourtier in the Val de Bagnes had often observed that erratic boulders in the plains were strikingly similar to boulders which he had seen on the glaciers, and which had apparently been transported by the glaciers from the point where they had fallen on to the ice from an adjacent mountain.

J. P. Perraudin (1767-1858) converted the Swiss civil engineer Venetz to his belief that a vast glacier had at one time extended down the valley of the Dranse to and beyond Martigny, and Venetz in due course convinced Charpentier. 'All honour,' writes

The Swiss and Their Mountains

W. A. B. Coolidge, 'to this humble observer "avant la lettre" whose name is briefly mentioned by Venetz (1812) and by Charpentier (1841)—both personal acquaintances of his—but his real merits have only recently been appreciated at their true worth value by Professor A. Forel, the great Swiss authority on glaciers.'[1]

Agassiz, once he was converted, lost no time in proclaiming his faith. Indeed, he was so prompt that Charpentier later accused him of stealing his ideas. On July 24, 1837, La Société Helvétique des Sciences Naturelles met at Neuchâtel under the presidency of Agassiz, who took as the theme for his opening paper the ancient extension of glaciers which, so he assured his startled audience, had once extended from the North Pole to Central Asia. Rarely has a paper read before a scientific society created a greater sensation. From that moment Agassiz was regarded as the originator of the theory of the glacial epochs, a position to which he had as much and as little claim as Darwin had to be the originator of the theory of evolution. The scepticism with which this theory was at first received incited Agassiz to search for more evidence in his support, and he spent five years studying glacier motion on the Unteraar glacier near the Grimsel. During this active period Agassiz, of course, felt it necessary to take on extra assistance. First there was Edward Desor, a political refugee who had taken a doctorate of science at Heidelberg. He was not only keenly interested in the new glacial theories, but he was also a mountaineer with a longer list of first ascents to his credit than any of the earlier mountaineers, with the single exception of Father Placidus. In 1841 Desor made the first ascent of the Ewigschnee-horn (10,929 feet), and with Agassiz the fourth of the Jungfrau (13,669 feet), the second of the Wetterhorn (Halse Jungfrau summit) (12,149 feet), the first ascent of the Rosenhorn peak of the Wetterhörner (12,110 feet), and the second of the Galenstock (11,802 feet). His books, *Excursions et séjours dans les glaciers* 1844 and *Nouvelles excursions et séjours dans les glaciers* . . . , were among the first books to contain descriptions of serious climbing in the Alps.

Another assistant was Karl Vogt. The nature of the stories exchanged between Desor and Vogt was one of Madame Agassiz's minor grievances, minor compared with the major

[1] *The Alps in Nature and History.* Methuen. Page 26.

96

17  PETER BIRMANN (1758–1844). Schreckhorn. Coloured copper engraving

grievance of shortage of funds and complete lack of privacy.

Dollfus Ausset, an Alsatian from Mulhausen, was Desor's companion on the Galenstock and Rosenhorn.

Gressly was a primitive type who had attracted Agassiz's attention by a brilliant essay on fossils. As he always slept in his clothes, and seldom changed them, he did not possess the minimum qualifications which would have entitled him to a bed in the Agassiz home, whenever such a bed happened to be vacant. Agassiz paid his modest expenses at a neighbouring inn. Though Gressly never had any money, he never seemed to need it, and this was perhaps his greatest charm for Agassiz. He lived in Neuchâtel in the winter, and in the summer tramped about the Jura searching for geological specimens, and apparently had no difficulty in exchanging amusing anecdotes for a bed. Tschudi took him with him on some mountain excursions. 'Apart from rocks,' wrote Tschudi, 'nothing in the world really seems to exist for him, and I really believe that if I were to break a fossilized shell I should reduce him to hysterical convulsions.'[1]

Such, then, was the staff of secretaries and assistants which Agassiz maintained, or occasionally failed to maintain, during the years which he devoted to glacier research. For most of them Mrs Agassiz had to provide meals, and usually at least one bed, and this in spite of the fact that she could have made good use of all available room after the arrival of her second child. The burden of housekeeping for this motley collection would have been sufficiently trying had they been less uncivilized as house guests, but they were impossible. They wandered about unkempt and unshaven, smoking stinking pipes, and with no subject of civilized conversation at meals, nothing but unending scientific shop.

And these were not the only people for whom Madame Agassiz was expected to find meals, for Agassiz thought nothing of dropping in with two or three chance acquaintances whom he had picked up on the road, and whose views on scientific subjects he had found interesting. Madame Agassiz not only house-kept for her husband in Neuchâtel but also in the 'Hôtel des Neuchâtelois' on the medial moraine on the Unteraar glacier near the Grimsel.

---

[1] 'Auser Steinen ist ihm nichts auf der Welt vorhanden, und ich glaube, durch Zerschlagen einer fossilen Muschel vor seinen Augen könnte man ihn zu hysterischen Konvulsionen bringen.' Schazmann, op. cit., page 20.

This 'hôtel' at first consisted of an overhanging boulder, the entrance to which was screened by a blanket. To satisfy Madame Agassiz, her husband eventually moved into even more palatial quarters, to wit, a rough cabin covered with canvas. 'The outer apartment,' complains Madame Agassiz, a lady hard to please, 'boasted a table and one or two benches; even a couple of chairs were kept as seats of honour for occasional guests. A shelf against the wall accommodated books, instruments, coats, etc; and a plank floor on which to spread their blankets at night was a good exchange for the frozen surface of the glacier.'

Madame Agassiz does not seem to have spent very long in this hôtel. Most of her summers during this period were spent with her parents and children in Germany.

In more recent times a club hut for mountaineers was built on the banks of the glacier very near the site of the 'Hôtel des Neuchâtelois' and was originally called the Pavilion Dollfuss, but the rebuilt club hut is now called the Lauteraar. Is there really any justification for this unfortunate change of name? The Alps owe much of their appeal to the patina of human associations, and one must therefore regret the discarding of a name which was a link with the historical associations of the Unteraar glacier.

During the five summers which Agassiz spent in this glacial refuge he made many interesting experiments. By driving stakes into the surface of the glacier and measuring their progress, he discovered that the centre of a glacier, like the centre of a river, moves faster than the sides; the sides, both of glacier and river, are slowed down by friction of the banks.

During these five years Agassiz made only two mountain ascents, the second ascent, and the first by amateurs, of the Wetterhorn, and the fourth of the Jungfrau. Agassiz was never a mountaineer in any real sense of the term, for his only interest in the mountains was scientific.

His name is commemorated by the Agassizhorn (3,953 m., 12,969 feet), a satellite of the Finsteraarhorn.

Neither Switzerland nor the Alps nor his family were powerful enough to keep Agassiz in Neuchâtel, once he had made up his mind to cross the Atlantic. America attracted him because he felt that there would be fascinating possibilities for scientific research in the new continent. He therefore gave up his position in Neuchâtel, and set out for the promised land with no prospects other than the remuneration from the Lowell Lectures which had been founded by a distinguished president of Harvard, and which he had been invited to deliver at the Lowell Institute in Boston. When I was asked to give these lectures in 1960, my appreciation of the honour was enhanced for me by the fact that among my predecessors were Agassiz and William James, a philosopher who had a very great influence on me in my youth.

Agassiz was thirty-eight years of age when he landed in America, and his confidence in his ability to establish himself in the New World was more than justified. America is the country of helpers, and when helpee meets helper, a good time is had by all. Agassiz was met in New York by John Lowell, who surrendered without a fight to his invincible charm, and before long Agassiz was appointed to the Faculty of Harvard.

'He came,' writes William James, 'in Byron's words, with victory beaming from his breast, and everyone went down before him, some yielding him money, some time, some specimens, and some labour, but all contributing their applause and their godspeed. And so, living among us from month to month and from year to year, with no relation to prudence except his pertinacious violation of all her usual laws, he on the whole achieved the compass of his desires, studied the geology and fauna of a continent, trained a generation of zoologists, founded one of the chief museums of the world, gave a new impulse to scientific education in America, and died the idol of the public, as well as of his circle of immediate pupils and friends.'[1]

After his appointment at Harvard, Agassiz realized that he would never again return to Switzerland. It was then that he decided to send for his family. Meanwhile his poor wife had died, and in due course Agassiz married a Boston lady, Elisabeth Cary, who had all the essential qualifications for this difficult post. She proved herself to be indeed a superb helper. Agassiz's luck held to the end, for his last day was spent in his beloved museum. He returned home feeling rather tired, and died in his sleep without waking and without pain. He died on December 12, 1873, in his sixty-seventh year. William James writes:

'Agassiz's influence on methods of teaching in our community

[1] William James: *Memories and Studies.* Longmans. Page 7.

was prompt and decisive—all the more so that it struck people's imagination by its very excess. The good old way of committing printed abstractions to memory seems never to have received such a shock as it encountered at his hands. There is probably no public school teacher who will not tell you how Agassiz used to lock a student up in a room full of turtle shells or lobster shells or oyster shells, without a book or word to help him, and not let him out till he had discovered all the truths which the objects contained. Some found the truths after weeks and months of lonely sorrow; others never found them. Those who found them were already made into naturalists thereby; the failures were blotted from the book of honour and of life. "Go to Nature; take the facts into your own hands; look and see for yourself"—these were the maxims which Agassiz preached wherever he went, and their effect on pedagogy was electric. . . ."[1]

[1] William James, *op. cit.*

# IO

## THE EARLY CLIMBERS

IN 1806 the first issue of *Alpina* was published in Winterthur, under the editorship of Carl Ulysses von Salis and Johann Rudolph Steinmüller. *Alpina*, which ceased publication four years later, was not a mountaineering journal. The first volumes contain articles on Alpine geology, Alpine vegetation, Alpine fauna and flora. True, there is also a description of the first ascent of the Ortler in 1804, an ascent the only interest of which for the editors of *Alpina* was the elaborate barometrical observations on the summit and in the valley to determine the height of the Ortler, incorrectly stated to be the third highest peak in the Alps, an error which provided unintended confirmation of an editorial comment. 'The Glockner and the Ortler,' wrote the editors, 'may be cited as striking examples of how little we knew, until recently, of the highest Alpine peaks. Quite apart from the Gotthard and Mont Blanc and their neighbouring peaks, there are still many marvellous and gigantic peaks which are as worthy of being better known.'

Later volumes of *Alpina* contain occasional reviews of books describing mountaineering expeditions, such as those by Bourrit and J. G. Ebel, but the conception of mountaineering *as a sport* was wholly unfamiliar to the editors.

It was not *Alpina* but the remarkable achievements of the Meyer family of Aarau which gave a great impetus to mountaineering in the first half of the nineteenth century.

### The Meyers
The Meyers were a family of well-to-do Aarau merchants. Johann Rudolf Meyer the first had climbed the Titlis above Engelberg in 1787 and crossed many of the lower passes, such as the Scheidegg, Grimsel and Furka. He must have been impressed by the inadequacy of the existing maps of the glacier regions and ambitious

to improve on them. What is certain is that he financed the publication of an atlas which contained by far the finest maps of the High Alps that had appeared until then. It was, indeed, one of Meyer's map surveyors, Herr Weiss from Strassburg, who was the first to reach the summit of the Oberaarjoch (10,607 feet). Modern skiers who ski over this pass in their hundreds would be amused by Herr Weiss's glowing description of its perils. Herr Weiss, according to Johann Rudolf Meyer the second, attained this pass only 'at the utmost risk of his life. He and his companions had to lower themselves into deep crevasses of the ice, and then try to find a way out again.'[1]

In 1788 the Hangendgletscherhorn (10,808 feet) had been climbed by J. E. Müller, one of Weiss's surveyors, who also sometime between 1792 and 1797 climbed the Uri Rothstock (9,620 feet).

In 1811 J. R. Meyer the second (1768-1825) and his brother Hieronymus picked up a porter, Abbühl, at Guttanen, crossed the Grimsel to the Valais, and made the first crossing of the Beich Pass (10,289 feet), a glacier pass which leads from Belalp above Brig to the Fafleralp at the head of the Lötschental. Here they reinforced their party by the addition of two chamois hunters, crossed the Lötschenlücke (10,512 feet) to the south-east foot of the Jungfrau (13,669 feet) which they climbed on August 3, 1811. They then recrossed the two above-mentioned passes, of both of which they had made the first traverse, and returned to the Oberland via the Grimsel. Not surprisingly their story was received with some scepticism, and it was therefore decided to repeat the ascent. Rudolf and Gottlieb Meyer, sons of J. R. Meyer the second, crossed the Oberaarjoch with two Valaisian chamois hunters, Alois Volker and Joseph Bortis, and the Guttanen porter[2] Arnold Abbühl. Here they separated. Rudolf and his guides reached the Gemslücke on the south-east ridge of the Finsteraarhorn. Meyer remained behind while the guides continued, and claimed to have reached the summit, a claim which, for reasons which we shall see, is no longer accepted.

[1] *Reise auf den Jungfrau-Gletscher und Ersteigung seines Gipfels, Joh. Rudolph Meyer und Hieronymus Meyer aus Aarau in Augustmonat 1811 unternommen,* Aarau 1812.
[2] Not a porter in the modern mountaineering sense of the term but a *knecht* or servant employed by a small inn.

On the following day the party crossed the Grünhornlücke (10,791 feet) where they were joined by Rudolf's brother Gottlieb (1793-1829). Next day, September 3rd, Gottlieb made the second ascent of the Jungfrau with the two Valaisian hunters. His brother Rudolf crossed the Oberaarjoch to the Unteraar glacier, and then made the first certain crossing of the Strahlegg pass (10,994 feet) to Grindelwald. The story of these remarkable climbs is told in *Reise auf den Jungfrau-Gletscher und Ersteigung seines Gipfels im August monat 1811* and *Reise auf die Eisgebirge des Kantons Bern und Ersteigung ihrer höchsten Gipfel im Sommer 1812*.

The Meyers were certainly outstanding among the pioneers of mountaineering. The great mountaineer and Alpine historian, Captain J. P. Farrar, pays a deserved tribute to them in the *Alpine Journal* (XXVII, p. 295).

'It has often seemed to me,' he writes, 'that the craft of mountaineering, and even more the art of mountaineering description, distinctly retograded for over fifty years after these great expeditions of the Meyers. It is not until the early sixties that rocks of equal difficulty are again attacked. Even then—witness Almer's opinion as to the inaccessibility of the Matterhorn—men had not yet learned the axiom, which Alexander Burgener was the first, certainly by practice rather than by explicit enunciation, to lay down, viz. that the practicability of rocks is only decided by actual contact. Meyer's guides had a glimmering of this. It is again not until the sixties that Meyer's calm yet vivid descriptions of actualities are surpassed by those brilliant articles of Stephen, of Moore, of Tuckett, and by Whymper's great *Scrambles* that are the glory of English Mountaineering.'

*Professor Franz Joseph Hugi (1796-1855)*
Hugi, a Soleure geologist, was a teacher of science by profession. In addition to his *Naturhistorische Alpenreise* (1830) and *Ueber das Wesen der Gletscher und Reise in das Eismeer* (1842), he defended in books and pamphlets his theories of glacier phenomena. Professor J. D. Forbes paid a notable tribute to Hugi's work as a glaciologist. 'He points out the correct method of observation, and though his work contains no accurate measurements he was perhaps the first who, by observing the

position of a remarkable block upon the Unteraar Glacier, indicated how such observations might be usefully made, instead of trusting (as appears to have been the former practice) to the vague report of the peasantry.'

In the early days of August 1828, Hugi made an attempt on the Jungfrau from Lauterbrunnen. On August 19th he made yet another unsuccessful attempt, this time on the Finsteraarhorn. On this occasion he reached the little saddle which now bears his name, the *Hugisattel* (4,084 m.), about 600 feet below the actual summit.

A year later, on August 10, 1829, Hugi took part in the first ascent of the Finsteraarhorn. He himself remained on the Hugisattel, but two of his guides, Jakob Leuthold and Johannes Währen, both from the Hasli valley in which Meiringen is situated, reached the actual summit where they built a cairn, fixing in it a pole to which they attached a flag, remnants of which were found when Herr J. Sulzer made the second ascent of the Finsteraarhorn in 1842. One of Hugi's guides, Arnold Abbühl, may perhaps have remained with him on the sattel. He certainly did not complete the ascent. It was this same Abbühl who had been one of Rudolf Meyer's guides when Meyer attempted the Finsteraarhorn in 1812. Meyer, as we have seen, remained behind on the ridge and sent the guides on. They claimed on their return to have reached the summit. During the course of the 1829 ascent, Hugi cross-examined Abbühl about the previous expedition, and under pressure Abbühl eventually admitted that none of Meyer's guides had reached the summit of the Finsteraarhorn. Hugi's expedition in 1829 is therefore now recognized to have been the first sucessful party to reach the summit of the Finsteraarhorn.

'It has been the custom,' wrote Captain J. P. Farrar, 'most unjustifiably to belittle Hugi's work as a mountaineer.' I too feel that Hugi has never received all the credit which he deserves. Nobody other than the present writer has recognized in Hugi the real father of winter mountaineering. He was in fact the first to penetrate into the High Alps in winter. In January 1832, Hugi spent two weeks in the Stieregg hut. His object was scientific. As the result of his expedition Hugi was able to disprove the theory, common at that period, that glaciers do not move in winter.

On January 8, 1832, Hugi started with eight herdsmen and chamois hunters, and with provisions for two or three weeks. He mentions Baumann (probably Peter), Burgener and Roth, '*der Felsenmann*'. The party with great trouble and danger reached at 3.30 p.m. the place where they supposed the Stieregg hut (5,742 feet) to be. They did not succeed in forcing an entrance before nightfall, and there in that small hut they remained for thirteen days, while Hugi made experiments on the movement of glaciers. On January 14th Hugi climbed the Strahlegg pass (10,994 feet). On January 16th he made an attempt to reach the Mönchjoch and penetrated as far as the great plateau below the Bergli rocks. On January 18th Hugi reached a point just below the Finsteraarjoch when the weather broke, and the whole party descended to Grindelwald by the Bäregg—a highly dangerous route. Two days later he ascended the Faulhorn in frosty weather, and remained in the summit hut three days.

Hugi published the results of his expeditions in the book to which reference has already been made. The ascent of the Strahlegg was the first expedition of its kind in winter, and proved what his summer climbs, perhaps, had failed to show—that Hugi was a mountaineer of unusual courage, originality and enterprise.

The Hugihorn (11,883 feet), a fine peak in the Schreckhorn group, perpetuates his name. This peak was first climbed and christened—appropriately enough—by one of the pioneers of winter mountaineering, Paul Montandon.

## Gottlieb Studer (1804-1890)

Gottlieb Studer of Berne was undoubtedly the most eminent mountaineer of the first half of the nineteenth century. His mountaineering career, which began in 1823, and which ended sixty years later in 1883, included no less than 643 distinct expeditions. Studer was essentially a mountain explorer rather than a specialist in the first ascent of difficult mountain peaks. He had climbed not only in the Swiss Alps but also in the Dauphiny, Graians and Tirol. In all these journeys he crossed passes some of which had never been crossed before, and others of which had only been crossed by natives.

Studer was a geologist and cartographer, and it was this common interest in the scientific and geographical aspects of mountain exploration which brought him and James Forbes together for an extended journey in the Valaisian Alps in the summer of 1842. Forbes's book, *Travels through the Alps of Savoy* (1843) was the first book in the English language to describe a series of climbs. After Studer and Forbes had separated, Forbes made the first recorded crossing of the Col d'Hérens and the first ascent of the Stockhorn (11,775 feet), now called the Wandfluhhorn, this being the first conquest of a virgin peak by a British mountaineer.

Studer, as I have said, was primarily a mountain explorer. He did make a number of first ascents of comparatively easy peaks, such as the Diablerets, and the first crossing of a number of easy glacier passes, but the conquest of difficult peaks for the sake of conquest did not appeal to him. He owes his distinguished place in Alpine history less to the numerous climbs which he made than to his outstanding contribution to our knowledge of the Swiss Alps. He drew no less than 710 mountain panoramas, by far the best mountain panoramas produced until then, and his maps of the southern valleys of the Valais (1849-53) were surprisingly good for the period. Finally, his comprehensive history of mountaineering in the Swiss Alps, *Über Eis und Schnee*, first issued in four volumes (1869-1883) with a new edition in three volumes (1896-1899) have proved invaluable to all subsequent Alpine historians. Many of Studer's explorations were made in company of Melchior Ulrich.

### Melchior Ulrich (1802-1893)
Melchior Ulrich was one of the earlier members of the Zürich school of climbing. His first climb was made in 1814 and his last in 1871. Ulrich's greatest achievement was the exploration from 1847 to 1852 of the glacier passes round Zermatt, of which very little was known at the time. His name is commemorated by the Urichshorn above Saas Fee.

### Johann Coaz (1822-1918)
Johann Coaz, the outstanding pioneer of mountaineering in the Engadine, began as a forest inspector, and was later employed to assist in collecting the topographical details for cartographers. It was as a cartographer that he made the first ascents of the Hoch-Ducan (10,060 feet) in 1845, Piz Kesch (11,221 feet) and Piz Lischanna (10,200 feet) in 1846, the Piz Uertsch (10,739

feet) and Piz dellas Calderas (11,132 feet) in 1847, the Piz Quater Vals (10,365 feet) in 1848, the Piz Mondin (10,325 feet), the Gemsbleisspitz, the Krone, the Piz Faschalba, the Augstenberg in 1849, the Piz Corvatsch (11,345 feet), Piz Güz, Piz Led (10,145 feet), Il Chapütschin (11,125 feet), Piz Misaun and Piz Tschierva (11,713 feet), all in 1850. Finally, on September 13, 1850, he made, with J. and Lorenz Ragut Tscharner, the first ascent of the monarch of the Engadine, the Piz Bernina (13,345 feet). This was a magnificent record.

## Balance Sheet 1850

There are peaks, such as the Wetterhorn, which are important irrespective of their relation to loftier neighbours, and there are other peaks, such as the Titlis and Dent du Midi which are important because they are the highest mountains dominating their respective valleys. In the following list of first ascents I have confined myself to peaks which were important for one or other of the above-mentioned reasons.

### First Ascents by the Swiss up to 1850

The following mountains were climbed by all-Swiss parties: Titlis, Mont Vélan, Dent du Midi, Dent de Morcles, Rheinwaldhorn, Uri-Rothstock, Oberalpstock, Jungfrau, Finsteraarhorn, Tödi, Altels, Oldenhorn, Sustenhorn, Wildhorn, Hasli Jungfrau (Wetterhorn), Il Chapütschin, Piz Corvatsch, Piz Misaun and Piz Bernina

### First Ascents by the Austrians up to 1850

The most notable climbs by the Austrians up to 1850 were the Grossglockner (1800), the Ortler (1804) to which perhaps might be added the Dachstein (1832).

### First Ascents by the French up to 1850

I include among the French the Chamoniards who were not French when they climbed Mont Blanc.

The difficult Mont Aiguille was climbed as far back as 1492, the Aiguille and Dôme du Goûter in 1784, Mont Blanc in 1786, the Aiguille de la Grande Sassière in 1810, the Zermatt Breithorn (by H. H. Maynard with Chamonix guides) in 1813, Mont Pelvoux, the Pyramid peak, in 1830, and Mont Pelvoux, the highest point, in 1848.

*First Ascents by the Italians up to 1850*
Rochemelon which, in spite of its height (11,611 feet), is snow-less and easy of access on its southern side and, crowned by a chapel, long a place of pilgrimage, was first ascended in 1358. The following first ascents were made in the Monte Rosa group, which until 1850 appears to have monopolized the attentions of enterprising Italian mountaineers: Punta Giordani (1801), Vincent Pyramid (1819), Zumsteinspitze (1820), Ludwigshöhe (1822) and the Signalkuppe of Monte Rosa (1842).

*First Ascents by the British up to 1850*
Prior to 1840 Coolidge, who tells us that he had 'taken some pains to look into the matter', could discover only meagre evidence of any climbs by the British. Mr Hill in 1786 reached the Col du Géant, and the pass was crossed by Mrs and Miss Campbell in 1822. Colonel Beaufoy climbed Mont Blanc in 1787, but J. D. Forbes was the first British subject to achieve a first ascent, the Stockhorn (11,796 feet) above the Col d'Hérens in 1842. It was not until 1845 that a really important virgin peak was climbed by a British mountaineer. It was in that year that a Scot, Stanhope Templeman Speer, made the first ascent of the Mittelhorn, the highest of the three Wetterhörner peaks.

*First Ascents by the Germans up to 1850*
Lauteraarhorn, Rosenhorn (Wetterhorn) and Ewigschneehorn.

To sum up. Up to and including 1850 the Swiss had incomparably the best record of the mountaineers of any country. And not only for mountaineering, but also for their contribution to our knowledge of the mountains. Simler, as we have seen, produced the first textbook on mountain craft, which was later brought up to date by Father Placidus. Gruner's *Die Eisgebirge des Schweizerlandes,* which was published in 1760, was the best book up to then of the region of the Alpine glaciers. Father Placidus produced some excellent maps. Agassiz might be described as the father of modern glaciology, and Studer the father of mountaineering history. Finally, General Dufour published between 1845 and 1865 twelve sheets of the famous Dufour map of the Swiss Alps.

Naturally the Swiss can hardly be congratulated on being the first to produce maps of their own mountains and glaciers, but the Dufour map was at the time the best mountain map produced by any country, and in some respect a model for all succeeding mountain maps. In honour of General Dufour the Swiss Government in 1863 named the highest point of Monte Rosa the Dufourspitze.

Such was the position in 1850, but within a few years the initiative had passed from the Swiss to the British. In the Golden Age of mountaineering which ended with the first ascent of the Matterhorn in 1865, of the thirty-nine major peaks first ascended during this period, no less than thirty-one were first ascended by British amateurs, most of whom were, of course, accompanied by Swiss guides.

The Alpine Club, which is the oldest of all mountaineering clubs, was founded in 1857, and the first volume of *Peaks, Passes and Glaciers* appeared in 1859. In 1863, the year in which the Swiss Alpine Club was founded, there appeared the first issue of the *Alpine Journal*, the world's oldest mountaineering journal, and John Ball's *Guide to the Western Alps*, the first guide book designed for mountaineers.

The only Swiss mountaineer during this period (1850-1863) who had a list of first ascents comparable to those of the leading members of the Alpine Club was the Bernese, Edmund von Fellenberg (1838-1902). His first ascents included the Weisse Frau peak of the Blümlisalp, the Doldenhorn, Silberhorn and Lauterbrunnen Breithorn. He reached the summit of the latter peak on July 31, 1865, a few minutes ahead of two famous English climbers, J. J. Hornby and T. H. Philpot. No mountaineer, amateur or professional, had a better knowledge of the Bernese Oberland, both from a mountaineering and from a geological point of view. Indeed, his mountaineering career from 1856 to 1883 was almost exclusively devoted to that region in which he had made more first ascents than any of the leading British mountaineers of the period.

## The Swiss Alpine Club

After the foundations of the Alpine Club on December 22, 1857, and of the Oesterreichischer Alpenverein in 1862, the Swiss mountaineers awoke to the fact that they had lost the initiative. On behalf of a large number of Swiss mountaineers who were determined that this state of affairs could not continue indefinitely, Dr Theodore Simler, a member of the Faculty of Berne University, issued a letter on October 21, 1862, which was sent to those Swiss mountaineers who were known to be interested in the foundation of a club. Dr Simler pointed out that unless steps were promptly taken, mountaineers who wanted information about the peaks and glaciers of Switzerland would have to consult the publications of the English Alpine Club, and this situation, he added, was not only troubling but definitely shaming. *'Eine solche Sachlage schien uns bemühend, ja sogar beschämend.'*

The Club was formally founded at a meeting held in Olten on April 19, 1863.

The fact that it was the British who founded the first Alpine Club is not altogether surprising. Man has been defined as a tool-making animal, and an Englishman might be defined as a club-making animal. The first thing the British did after establishing a base in some remote African or Asiatic colony was to found a club. The organization of sport in 1850 was more developed in Great Britain than in any other country.

Clubs which claim to represent a particular sport may be either exclusive or inclusive. The Royal Yacht Squadron and the Jockey Club are examples of exclusive clubs, the Swiss Alpine Club of an inclusive club.

The Alpine Club was from the first exclusive rather than inclusive. It was restricted to experienced mountaineers, and every candidate was, and is still, required to submit to the Committee a list of the peaks and passes which he has climbed. The great advantage of an inclusive club is that its financial resources are necessarily far greater than those of exclusive clubs. The only service which the Alpine Club as such could render to the general body of mountaineers was the publication of the *Alpine Journal*, and of the excellent series of Alpine guides, the first volumes of which were written by John Ball. The Swiss Alpine Club, on the other hand, has rendered outstanding services to mountaineers in general and not only to Swiss mountaineers. It has raised the necessary funds to build club huts throughout the Alps, and in addition the SAC has published excellent climbers' guides for the use not only of summer climbers but also of ski-mountaineers. It is under their auspices that the examinations for the guide's certificate are conducted.

British mountaineers have contributed to this good work by becoming members of the Swiss Alpine Club, but there was a strong feeling at the beginning of this century that the British as such should make their own particular contribution to the building of club huts. A special Association was founded by Mr J. A. B. Bruce for British members of the Swiss Alpine Club, and it was this Association which collected funds to build the Britannia Hut above Saas Fee in 1912. There are, of course, Swiss clubs organized on an exclusive basis, the Academic Alpine Clubs of Berne and Zürich for instance, the nurseries of some of the most famous climbers of today.

It may be of of interest for some readers to know that the Ski Club of Great Britain began by modelling itself on the Alpine Club, and by demanding technical and social qualifications, and ended by modelling itself on the Swiss Alpine Club. It is an inclusive organization of which the membership at the time of writing is nearly 15,000. The Alpine Ski Club, on the other hand, is, like the academic mountaineering clubs, a small club with little over a hundred members which only admits experienced mountaineers.

# II

## A CENTURY OF SWISS MOUNTAINEERING

FROM THE beginnings of mountaineering until 1850 the Swiss amateurs, as I have shown, had a better record than the mountaineers of any other country, but after 1850 they lost the initiative. Fellenberg was the last outstanding Swiss amateur of the nineteenth century. The guides who led the majority of the first ascents in the second half of the century were Swiss, but their employers were seldom Swiss.

In his survey of 'modern mountaineering' in *The Alps in Nature and History,* which was published in 1908, W. A. B. Coolidge, an erudite Alpine historian, appears to consider that only two Swiss mountaineers between 1865 and 1908 are worthy of mention, Eugène Rambert and Emile Javelle. Rambert was mainly important as an historian, and certainly his *Alpes Suisses,* issued in five volumes between 1866 and 1875, and reissued in six volumes (1887-1889) was a valuable contribution to Alpine literature. Emile Javelle (1847-1883) was a Frenchman by birth and a Swiss by adoption. He made the first ascent of the Tour Noire in 1876, and an early ascent, the 17th, of the Matterhorn, the only ascent, incidentally, in 1870, but his record as a mountaineer was not in the same class as that of the best contemporary British climbers. He did, however, make a fine contribution to Alpine literature, *Souvenirs d'un Alpiniste* (1886), of which an English translation, *Alpine Memories,* was published in London in 1889.

It is odd that Coolidge did not mention Dr Dübi, because they collaborated at one time in the production of climbers' guides, and Dübi must have been one of the few Alpine writers of distinction with whom Coolidge did not quarrel. Dr Dübi spoke at Coolidge's funeral, at which I was present. He referred to their long partnership in Alpine research and to Coolidge's distinction as the first historian who specialized in Alpine history, a tribute which Bourrit's ghost may have resented, but he admitted that

18 MAXIMILIEN DE MEURON (1785–1868). The source of the Rhone. Coloured copper engraving

his old friend had a difficult side to his nature, and was apt to be a trifle *schroff* in the written word.

Dr Heinrich Dübi made some fine expeditions in his youth, among them the first ascent of the Allalinhorn from the North East by the East ridge, and the discovery of the true route up the Jungfrau from the Rottal, but his great contribution to mountaineering was in the field of history and guide books. He edited the *Jahrbuch* of the Swiss Alpine Club from 1891 to 1923, and his Climbers' Guides for the Bernese Oberland are a model of patient research. His other works include the second edition of Gottlieb Studer's *Über Eis und Schnee* and innumerable articles on Alpine pioneers. But perhaps his most valuable contribution to Alpine history was his monograph *Paccard wider Balmat* which was, as we have seen, one of the first real efforts to get the record straight. He was born in 1848 and died in 1942.

The revival of enterprising climbing by Swiss amateurs seems to have approximately synchronized with the foundation of the Swiss university climbing clubs, the Akademischer Alpen-Club Zürich (AACZ) in 1896 and the Akademischer Alpen-Club Berne (AACB) in 1907. These small clubs only admitted climbers who would add to the strength of a guideless party attempting difficult ascents. During the last decade of the nineteenth and the first decade of the twentieth century it was a member of the AACB, Gustav Hasler, who was perhaps the best Swiss amateur. With the guide Fritz Amatter of Grindelwald, who later led the Japanese Yuko Maki on the first ascent of the Mitteleggi ridge of the Eiger, Hasler made the first ascent of the great North-East wall of the Finsteraarhorn, direct to the summit. This was the first of the classic North wall ascents which are the speciality of modern experts.

It was between the wars that the Swiss amateurs again became pre-eminent in the pioneering of new routes. Hans Lauper of the Akademischer Alpen-Club Berne was one of the most expert amateurs of the period. With Max Liniger he made in 1921 the first ascent of the North face of the Mönch, with Pierre von Schumacher in 1926 the first direct ascent of the North face of the Jungfrau, and in 1932 with that brilliant Swiss mountaineer, Alfred Zürcher,[1] and two famous guides, Joseph Knubel and

---

[1] In its centenary year the Alpine Club elected two foreign Vice-Presidents, Count Aldo Bonacossa and Alfred Zürcher.

Alexander Graven, the first ascent of the North face of the Eiger. My comments on this great climb must be deferred until I have mentioned some of the many remarkable *first* ascents made by Swiss climbers between the two world wars.

Among them the following were perhaps the most note-worthy: the North face of the Lauterbrunnen Breithorn (Daniel Chervet and Willy Richardet), the North face of the Aiguille de Triolet (André Roch and Robert Gréloz), the Fiescherhorn by the Fiescherwand (Walter Amstutz and Pierre von Schumacher) and the West face of the Schreckhorn by Dr Oskar Hug.

A brilliant first ascent, which for some reason did not attract the attention which it deserved, was of the difficult South face of the Jungfrau by Ernst Gertsch and Fritz Fuchs of Wengen. Ernst Gertsch, his brother Eduard and Fritz Fuchs were already known for what the *Alpine Journal* described as 'their brilliant ascent in 1926 of the Rotbrett arête of the Jungfrau'. The South face of the Jungfrau was first climbed in 1927 as late as November 6th.

It is curious how few mountaineers are aware of the fine climbs, mainly carried out between the wars, by the inhabitants of Mürren. Ernst Feuz's achievement in discovering new routes up Oberland faces rivals that of the famous German climber, Willi Welzenbach.

In 1934 Ernst Feuz and Walter von Allmen climbed the North face of the Grosshorn by a more direct and more difficult route than Welzenbach's. In 1936 the same partners made two splendid ascents in the Lötschental (the North face of the Lötschentaler Breithorn and the North face of the Breitlauihorn).

In 1940 Feuz and Emil von Allmen of Mürren made a new route up the North face of the Lauterbrunnen Breithorn via the West ridge. Feuz finally rounded off his magnificent series of new Oberland routes by the first ascents of the North face of the Tschingelgrat and Tschingelspitz, his companions being Walter von Allmen and Hermann Salvisberg.

In July 1947 Emil von Allmen of Mürren with Willi Roth of Berne made the first ascent of the difficult South wall of the Gspaltenhorn, a splendid climax to the achievements of the Mürren group.

## The North face of the Eiger

The North face of the Eiger is the highest cliff in the Alps, rising

1,800 metres from the grass slopes to the Eiger crest. It is divided into two clearly defined parts, the North-East face which Lauper climbed, and the North-West face, first climbed in 1938 by two German and two Austrian climbers.

The ridge which divides the Lauper route from the so-called Eiger North face route also marks the division between the classic and the most extreme modern conception of mountaineering. The Lauper route is almost free from objective dangers. Not one piton or other artificial climbing aid was used on the first ascent. The Harrer route will always involve great objective dangers such as falling stones and snow slides and the perils of storm if the weather changes. Colonel E. L. Strutt, an ultra-conservative, in his valedictory address as President of the Alpine Club delivered on December 7, 1938, described the Eigerwand as 'the most imbecile variant since mountaineering began'. Lauper and Zürcher were both members of the Alpine Club, and though neither of them would have expressed themselves as strongly as Strutt, they did not deviate in their climbs from the classic tradition. Lauper never used pitons, and watched with increasing misgiving the approach of what has been called the Iron Age of Mountaineering. He was only forty when he died.

*Othmar Gurtner*

The Eiger controversy inevitably recalls to my mind an old and valued friend, Othmar Gurtner, for the last article which he contributed to The Mountain World was a well-documented account of all the North face climbs, and a strong attack on the Eigerwand route as altogether unjustifiable. By the time he wrote, seventeen climbers had lost their lives. His verdict did not differ materially from Colonel Strutt's.

Othmar Gurtner was born at Lauterbrunnen in 1895 and died at Zürich in 1958. He soon became an expert mountaineer and skier. He made a name as a sporting journalist, and in the twenties he was a convincing and influential champion of the British campaign for the recognition of Downhill and Slalom ski-racing. Ski races, in spite of the speed, are often dull to watch and usually even duller to read about. Gurtner could dramatise what was interesting, and his astringent wit, sometimes faintly touched with innocent malice, often gave pain to serious-minded officials and organizers of races, whose defects he took an impish delight in exposing. As a result, *Sport* (Zürich), of which he was the ski-ing correspondent, was read with delight by the public and by the select minority of ski officials whose more sensitive corns had not attracted his agile foot.

## Retrospect 1863-1963

This book, as I explained in the preface, does not claim to be a history either of the Swiss Alpine Club or of Swiss mountaineers, for I have had within the limits of my space to discuss many other aspects of the relations between the Swiss and their mountains. Had I been able to devote more space to the Swiss mountaineers, there are many whose achievements I should have chronicled in addition to those who have been mentioned, however briefly, in the previous chapters. It would, for instance, be impossible to omit in any adequate history of the Swiss Alpine Club all mention of such distinguished climbers as Hans Biehly, E. R. Blanchet, Julien Gallet, Charles Gos, Robert Gréloz, Hans Koenig and Georg Leuch.

Moreover, though I have tried to mention the more outstanding climbs in the great ranges of Asia and the American continent, I could not within the limits of this chapter do full justice to all the achievements of Swiss mountaineers in the Caucasus, in the Pamir and Tian Schan, in New Zealand and in the Rockies. And I can only allow myself a fleeting reference to that great Genevese explorer Mlle Kini Maillart.

In the Himalayas, the Swiss did not achieve any of the four supreme prizes of Himalayan exploration, Everest, Kanchenjunga, K2 or Nanga Parbat, but they succeeded twice in climbing the highest of the mountains unclimbed at the time of their ascent, Lhotse and Dhaulagiri.

The contribution of Swiss mountaineers to the exploration of the Alps may be summed up as follows:

From the beginnings of mountaineering to 1850 the Swiss had a far longer list of Alpine first ascents to their credit than the mountaineers of any other country. In the second half of the nineteenth century, the majority of first ascents were led by Swiss guides, but the role of the Swiss amateurs was inconspicuous.

In the twentieth century the crack mountaineers laid siege to the great North walls of Alpine peaks. Of these the most important were undoubtedly the North walls of the Finsteraarhorn, Eiger, Mönch, Jungfrau (direct ascent), which were first climbed by Swiss, the North walls of the Matterhorn by Germans, the Piz Badile and Grandes Jorasses by Italians and the Eigerwand by a German-Austrian party. There were, of course, many other difficult climbs in this period, but these were the outstanding achievements.

Now we may divide these North face climbs either into those which were climbed by Swiss and those which were climbed by non-Swiss, or into those which were climbed by the traditional methods and those which were climbed with artificial aids, pitons, etc. And we shall note with interest that these groups coincide, for the North faces climbed without artificial aids were all climbed by the Swiss. The remaining North faces were more difficult, and probably unclimbable by the traditional methods. Briefly, the Swiss in this period approached the limit of what was climbable by the traditional methods.

To sum up, if we take into account as we must, the great contribution of Swiss guides to the exploration not only of the Alps but also of distant ranges, the record of Swiss mountaineers, amateurs and professionals, compares favourably with what was accomplished by the mountaineers of other countries.

*Ski-ing*
Of the pioneers of ski-mountaineering none had a more distinguished record than Marcel Kurz of Neuchâtel and F. Roget of Geneva. Their outstanding achievements are recorded in my books *A History of Ski-ing, The Story of Ski-ing* and *A Century of Mountaineering.*

Switzerland is the cradle of the Alpine forms of ski competition. The traditional Scandinavian competitions are the Cross-country and the Jumping, and it was perhaps inevitable that the Alpine peoples should have blindly copied the type of race which developed naturally out of Scandinavian terrain instead of experimenting with forms of racing more suitable to the Alps. It was the British, and notably the members of the Kandahar Ski Club, which pioneered the Alpine forms of ski-racing, Downhill and Slalom. The modern Slalom, which the present writer invented, bears much the same relation to the old Norwegian Slalom that speed skating bears to figure skating. Our first continental ally in our attempt to secure international recognition for Downhill and Slalom racing was Dr Walter Amstutz, and the Anglo-Swiss University race which he and I inaugurated is the oldest international event in Downhill and Slalom racing.

# 12

## THE EVOLUTION OF THE ALPINE GUIDE

BEFORE mountaineering developed as a sport, the Berglers, as the natives of mountain valleys describe themselves, mastered such elementary mountaincraft as was necessary for chamois hunting or smuggling, and in some valleys, such as Zermatt, through which an occasional traveller passed on the way to Italy, there were always some Berglers who knew enough about glaciers and snowfields to guide them over the Théodule glacier pass. Berglers in fact have crossed passes and wandered about mountains in search of chamois from time immemorial, but they crossed passes for practical reasons; no Bergler climbed peaks merely for the fun of climbing them. That they themselves attached little importance to the conquest of virgin peaks emerges very clearly from the story of an attempt on the unconquered Mönch by a Rumanian Countess, Hélène Kolzow-Massalsky, better known under her pen name of Dora d'Istria. After spending a miserable night in a cave, the Countess was propelled upwards by the combined efforts of four guides, one for each arm, one to push behind and one to pull from in front. The Countess collapsed at the foot of the final snow ridge of the Mönch and abandoned the ascent.

Now there was not one of these guides who could not have collected a party of friends and completed the ascent of the as yet unconquered Mönch, but it was not until two years later that Christian Almer, who had been one of the Countess's party, made the first ascent of the Mönch with Dr Porges of Vienna. Why did Almer allow two years to pass before returning to the point where the Countess had collapsed and himself completing the ascent? Probably because it would have been regarded as eccentric for a Bergler to climb a peak for fun, and not only eccentric but improvident to spoil the market by reducing the number of virgin peaks for the conquest of which a grateful Herr would pay his guides generously.

119

When Alfred Wills climbed the Wetterhorn, not only his guides but the village conspired to make him believe that he was making the first ascent. The village fêted him on his return, and yet many of the villagers must have known that his guide, Peter Bohren, had climbed the Wetterhorn twice, perhaps three times, before he had led Wills to the summit and encouraged him to believe that he was, in Wills's words, 'the first to scale that awful peak'. Few indeed were the first ascents made by Berglers who were not paid for their services. The first ascent of the Wetterhorn proper, the Hasli Jungfrau, was admittedly made by two guides, M. Bannholzer and J. Jaun, on August 31, 1844, but those guides were not climbing for the fun of the thing. They had been paid by Desor to find the way to the summit, and Desor himself followed a few days later.

In my book *A Century of Mountaineering* I devoted a chapter to the great guides of the Golden Age, Christian Almer, Melchior Anderegg, Ulrich Lauener, Michel Croz and J. A. Carrel. Of these, Carrel certainly explored the great Italian ridge of the Matterhorn with some friends from the valley, but in this he would seem to have been exceptional. I am not, of course, suggesting that the guides only climbed for money and derived no particular pleasure from climbing. To plan and lead a difficult first ascent is an exacting test not only of physical but also of intellectual qualities, and is indeed one of the most rewarding experiences in sport, whether the leader be a professional guide or an amateur. Why then did not guides in the Golden Age make up a party of Berglers and climb a virgin peak just for the fun of climbing it?

I am not sure that the guides themselves could have given a clear answer to this question. Mountain people are often governed by implicit rather than by explicit rules of behaviour, by those laws which, as Thucydides observes, 'because they are unwritten are the most shameful to break'. Climbing mountains for sport was, as the Berglers realized, an invention of the foreign tourists whose holidays were short and whose opportunities were limited. It would therefore perhaps have been not quite correct, or as we should say, not quite sporting, for Berglers who had unlimited opportunities to climb their own peaks, to make up parties on their own and clean up the remaining virgin peaks just for their own amusement. Moreover, it would be bad business.

For the amateur the problem was to make a first ascent. For

19 MOUNTAINEER'S DRESS AT THE END OF THE 18TH CENTURY. Copper engraving
from Joh. Gottfried Ebel, «Anleitung die Schweiz zu bereisen», Zurich 1804

20 THE FIRST INN ON RIGIKULM, erected 1816, with early Rigi travellers. Contemporary coloured lithography

21 WEDDING PARTY AND TOURISTS ON RIGIKULM. Woodcut around 1860 after
a humouristic drawing by H. Jenny

22  HOTEL RHONEGLETSCHER AND THE NEW FURKA ROAD. Woodengraving from
an illustrated paper around 1870

the guide the problem was more complex. He had first to persuade some keen amateur to engage him, and then to lead that
amateur up a virgin peak. His status in the hierarchy of guides
was determined by the status of his employers, for the keenest
and most enterprising amateurs only employed the best guides.

## The Relation of Amateur and Guide

The proportions in which the credit for a first ascent should be
shared between the amateur and the guide varies from case to
case. Stephen's ironic belittlement of his own contribution to
virgin ascents erred on the side of modesty.

'I utterly repudiate the doctrine,' he writes, 'that Alpine
travellers are or ought to be the heroes of Alpine adventures. The
true way at least to describe all my Alpine ascents is that Michel
or Anderegg or Lauener succeeded in performing a feat requiring
skill, strength and courage, the difficulty of which was much increased by the difficulty of taking with him his knapsack and his
employer. If any passages in the succeeding pages convey the
impression that I claim any credit except that of following better
men than myself with decent ability, I disavow them in advance
and do penance for them in my heart.'

There were, of course, amateurs of whom this was true,
W. A. B. Coolidge for instance, who had great pluck and en-
durance, but who was unathletic and short-sighted and who
could not have led a guideless party up the easiest of mountains.
Some of the pioneers were almost as unathletic as Coolidge, and
such amateurs naturally tended to be uncritical in praise of their
guides. There were indeed very few outstanding athletes among
the British pioneers, for the outstanding athlete tends to devote
all his spare time to the game or sport of his choice. Richard
Barrington was an exception. He had ridden the winner of the
Irish Grand National, a far more exacting test of courage and
balance and skill than following a guide up an Alpine peak. His
first peak was the Jungfrau, and he was unimpressed.

'I met some Alpine men whose footsteps I had tracked down
the glacier. Talking about climbing I said to them I did not think
much of the work I had done, and was answered : "Try the Eiger
or the Matterhorn." "All right," I said. . . . Started at 3.30 a.m.
on August 11th for the Eiger. We took a flag from the hotel.
When we came to the point where one descends into a small

hollow, I looked well with my glass over the face of the Eiger next us, and made up my mind to try the rocks in front. . . . Almer and Bohren said it was no use, and declined to come the way I wished. "All right," I said, "you may stay; I will try." So off I went for about 300 or 400 yards over some smooth rocks to the part which was almost perpendicular. I then shouted and waved the flag for them to come on, and after five minutes they followed and came up to me. They said it was impossible. I said: "I will try." So with the rope coiled over my shoulders, I scrambled up, sticking like a cat to the rocks, which cut my fingers, and at last got up say 50 to 60 feet. I then lowered the rope, and the guides followed with its assistance.'

This was an extreme case, but the great guides who made their reputations during the Golden Age began as chamois hunters or smugglers, and some of them learned as much from their employers as they taught them. Uncritical praise of the guides inevitably led to uncritical depreciation, as, for instance, in the following passage by Claire Eliane Engel:[1]

'However sacrilegious it may sound, the worst adversaries of mountaineering were the guides. Much has been written about them, and most texts fall little short of hagiography. And yet as soon as modern mountaineering began, guides did everything in their power for various reasons to oppose it. To climb the Aiguille Verte was obviously more tiring and dangerous than to go to the Jardin de Talèfre. Devising new climbs required imagination and foresight. Now it is a fact that not only were hardly any routes discovered by local peasants unless prompted or led by tourists, but they usually did much to prevent tourists having their own way.'

This was only true of second and third class guides, and if an enterprising amateur employed such guides he had only himself to blame for lack of success. First-class guides have always been and still are the exception. As Ronald Clark rightly says in his excellent book, *The Early Alpine Guides*, 'the claim that there are not more than few dozen first-class guides runs like an unbroken sigh through the climbing literature of the sixties and seventies. C. E. Mathew in his great monograph on Mont Blanc

[1] *A History of Mountaineering*, London, p. 137.

insisted "that of the three hundred men now (1898) on the Chamonix roll those who could be relied on in a grave emergency may be counted almost on the fingers of one hand".'

As an example of what Dr Engel calls texts which 'are little short of hagiography', the following may be cited from the Badminton Volume on *Mountaineering* (1892) by Clinton Dent, a past President of the Alpine Club.

'It is on rocks alone that an amateur can and must exercise his own powers, and not be wholly dependent on his guides. On snow, the amateur is but an impediment, an extra burden, as has often been said, to his guides; they have to hack out huge steps for his benefit; he is entirely dependent on them for steering clear of avalanches, rotten snow-bridges and the like.'

To sum up: the greatest guides of the Golden Age made a notable contribution to mountaineering. Few indeed were the amateurs who could have led a guideless party on an important first ascent, and those who could have done so did not realize their powers, and acquiesced in the tradition that guides were essential. But, then as now, first-class guides were rare, and there were many third-class guides whose attitude was not unfairly described in the passage which I have quoted from Dr Engel.

*Christian Klucker and the new outlook*
Christian Klucker (1853-1928) was perhaps the greatest of the many great guides who were natives of the Engadine. His first ascents included the great Peuterey ridge of Mont Blanc, the North East face of the Lyskamm, the North face of the Piz Roseg and Piz Tschierva, the North East face of the Piz Bernina, many fine new climbs in the Forno Albigna and, in the Dolomites, the North face of the Fünffingerspitze. His outlook was different from that of most of his predecessors. There is little to suggest that the guides of the Golden Age of mountaineering, which is considered to have ended with the ascent of the Matterhorn, ever read the descriptions of their expeditions, written by the amateurs whom they guided. Indeed, they seem to have been content that the main credit for these climbs should be given to their employers.

Klucker was different. He read with interest, and sometimes with disapproval, articles on the climbs which he had led. He bitterly resented the attitude of one of his employers, a Russian mountaineer, Anton von Rydzewski, who seemed to have expected 'servility and drawing-room etiquette'.[1]

'The further recognition,' writes Klucker, 'that Rydzewski in his articles desires to pose as initiator, so to speak, of our new enterprises, was also distasteful to me, because it does not represent the facts by a long way.'

To the end of his life Klucker kept up his great interest in Alpine literature, and he corresponded frequently with Captain J. P. Farrar. 'In each man,' writes Tyndale, 'lay a deep love of mountains, the scholar's enthusiasm for Alpine history in its minutest details, and the ever-ready wish to help the younger generation.' 'There has been no better mountaineer,' wrote Farrar in Klucker's *Führerbuch*, 'he will go down in Alpine history as practically without a rival for supreme knowledge of a mountain, never-failing care, executive ability and a sterling character that makes him a charming companion.'

*The end of a chapter*
A chapter, if not an epoch, ended with the outbreak of the First World War. Prior to 1914 the best guides were still in a different class from the best amateurs. In the closing years of that period the most successful partnership between an outstanding guide and an outstanding amateur was the partnership between Geoffrey Winthrop Young and Joseph Knubel. In his descriptions of their most famous climbs, Geoffrey Young made it clear that he could not have led the occasional pitch which extended even Knubel's fantastic powers to their utmost, notably the Knubel pitch on the direct ascent of the Mer de Glace face of the Grépon, but Young's contribution to this and other great climbs was important, for it was Young who invented and planned many of their most daring virgin ascents. Knubel was a superb tactician, and a brilliant rock climber, but he was no strategist. He was therefore the ideal partner for a gifted amateur who would not have been satisfied unless he too had made his own contribution to the solution of a mountain problem. Knubel was not only a great summer guide; he had also to his credit a longer list of first ski ascents than any other guide.

[1] *Adventures of an Alpine Guide* by Christian Klucker. Translated from the German edition. Edited by H. E. G. Tyndale. John Murray. Pp 109 and 114.

Perhaps the greatest guide of this period was Franz Loch-matter. Young's description of the first ascent of the South face of the Täschhorn in a storm is one of the classics of Alpine litera-ture. Even modern experts find the worst pitches on that climb extremely severe in good weather. Nobody but Lochmatter could have saved the party. The amateurs Ryan and Young only climbed the pitch which Lochmatter led with the maximum of assistance from the rope. Lochmatter's lead on that occasion still seems to me the greatest single achievement in mountaineering history.

*The status of the guides between the two World Wars*
Whereas prior to 1914 the best amateurs were quite definitely inferior to the best guides, there was no similar disparity during the period between the two World Wars. Franz and Toni Schmid, who made the first ascent of the North face of the Matterhorn, Willi Welzenbach, who led a series of North face climbs in the Oberland, R. Cassin, who made the first ascent of the North face of the Grandes Jorasses direct to Pointe Walker, were the equal of the best guides of the period. The same is true of many amateurs today.

*The guide as amateur*
The word 'amateur' is derived from *amo*, 'I love', and a guide who will accompany friends unpaid for the love of mountaineer-ing obviously has his amateur side. There are, of course, varying degrees of amateurism in the rather special sense in which I use this word in this particular context. A guide may lead a party in an unpaid capacity as legitimate advertisement for his skill, and in the hope, if he makes a notable first ascent, of attracting the kind of client whom he desires. Or he may make a first ascent alone and then lead a client to the summit, as did Armand Charlet who made the first ascent of L'Isolée des Aiguilles du Diable (Mont Blanc) and then led E. R. Blanchet to the summit without apparently letting him know that the peak was no longer virgin.[1]

This was not, I feel, conscious deceit. Through the nineteenth century and during the early decades of this century, many guides seemed to have believed in all good faith that a first ascent

[1] Blanchet, *Hors des Chemins battus*, pp. 191-221.

by guides alone did not count. Perhaps they subscribed to Conway's dogma: 'unrecorded ascents don't count'. Much the same principle seems to have been applied to first ascents where a guide, acting in an unpaid capacity, led some natives of his own village on a first ascent. Thus Sydney Spencer made in 1894 what he believed to be the first winter ascent of the Dom, only to discover later that one of his guides had climbed the Dom in winter with some friends from his village.

Walter Risch made a solitary first winter ascent of Piz Scerscen by the Nase. The brother Supersaxo made first ski ascents round Saas Fee without tourists. Prominent among the guides who climbed for fun were Armand Charlet, Emilio Comici, who made the first ascent of the North Face of the Cima Grande di Lavaredo, Gaston Rébuffat, Cesare Maestri and Walter Bonatti.

The amateur guides, by which I mean guides who often climbed as unpaid members of a party, were prominent in what Marcel Kurz calls the fourth phase of the conquest of the Alps, making new routes in winter. Winter mountaineering is now regarded as the best training for Himalayan expeditions.

In the Oberland amateur guides have achieved some very fine climbs. Fritz Fuchs who accompanied Ernst Gertsch on the first ascent of the South face of the Jungfrau (page 114), came along as a friend without being paid. Adolf Rubi of Grindelwald and Hans Schlunegger of Wengen provided a startling demonstration of the speed at which first-class guides can move. On July 1, 1935, starting from the Mittellegi Hut on the Eiger, they traversed in succession Eiger, Mönch and Jungfrau (by the very difficult East ridge) and reached Stechelberg, climbing for only sixteen hours and ten minutes. Karl Schlunegger and Otto von Allmen, both guides, made the direct ascent of the North face of the Wengern Jungfrau, the most difficult of the Jungfrau climbs.

### The modern guide

In the first decade of this century it would have been very difficult for a ski-teacher to earn ten francs a day but fairly easy for a guide to earn twenty-five or thirty francs a day. Thus the tariff for the Wetterhorn, a two-day climb, was sixty francs. Today the best ski-teachers earn seventy francs a day, and it is easy for any competent ski-teacher to earn fifty francs a day, which is approximately the same as a guide earns who devotes two days to the ascent of the Wetterhorn, for which he is now paid 110 francs.

Now the guide who leads his client up the Wetterhorn has to climb 9,000 feet from the valley and carry a heavy sack and prepare the meals for his client in the club hut. The ski-teacher, on the other hand, does his climbing in a ski lift and seldom carries a sack. Finally, the Wetterhorn, though an easy mountain, is from time to time the scene of a fatal casualty. In brief, the ski-teacher earns his money far more easily than the guide.

Since the end of the First World War even the best of guides could not make a living out of guiding *alone*. The standard of climbing among amateurs has risen fantastically since 1914, and amateurs who are good enough to attempt the most severe climbs seldom take guides. Consequently, it is only the exceptional guide who benefits by that continuous practice on difficult climbs, without which a mountaineer cannot remain in the top class. Whereas in my youth the highest compliment which one could pay to an amateur was to describe him as '*almost* as good as a first-class guide', I recently heard a Swiss friend of mine remark, without irony, that a certain guide was 'as good as the best amateur'.

Indeed, most of the post-war cracks have been amateurs. There remains a small élite of guides who continue to be engaged for the severest of climbs, among them Hermann Steuri who made the second ascent of the North face of the Matterhorn and who, in his day, was a member of the Swiss ski team. Steuri undergoes severe training before the beginning of the climbing season, for only a guide who is in perfect condition can safely lead the most exacting of modern climbs.

Steuri made his name before the Second World War, Hilti von Allmen of Lauterbrunnen is one of the outstanding guides of the younger generation. As a machine mechanic he was earning good money, 1,500 Swiss francs (£125) a month, when the call of the mountains proved too strong. He became a professional, as the only way of continuing to practise the art he loved, and indeed made a real financial sacrifice to adopt this profession. For two summers he spent his savings to familiarize himself with the Alps from end to end, from the Calanques near Marseilles to the Gasäuse near Vienna, climbing as an unpaid amateur with friends. Again in 1961 he climbed the Eigerwand with a friend.

Finally, on February 4, 1962, Hilti von Allmen and his friend, Paul Etter, a miner from Walenstadt, succeeded in making the first winter ascent of the North face of the Matterhorn. Hilti von Allmen is also a first-class ski-teacher.

There can be no sport in which the relations between a great amateur and a great professional is nobler than the relationship between amateur and guide at its best. What that bond can mean emerges from the most moving tribute ever paid by an amateur to a guide, Captain J. P. Farrar's tribute to Daniel Maquinaz: 'There are many among my contemporaries who will understand the feelings of more than ordinary friendship that binds one to a man like this whom one has learned to know and to judge in that school of stern, though voluntary, discipline and not infrequent danger that is of the essence of serious mountaineering. I lose in him one from whom I learned much—from whom I never ceased to learn—my leader on many a glorious day of triumph—one whose memory will in my mind for ever be entwined with some of the most unsullied and serene joys that enter into the life of man.'

23   ALEXANDRE CALAME (1810–1864). Rosenlaui with Wellhorn and Wetterhorn.
Oil (private property)

## 13

## MOUNTAIN FORTRESS

---

*Prime Minister to Foreign Secretary*                    *3 Dec., 44*
'I put this down for the record. Of all neutrals Switzerland has
the greatest right to distinction. She has been the sole international force linking the hideously sundered nations and our-
selves. What does it matter whether she has been able to give
us the commercial advantages we desire or has given too many
to the Germans, to keep herself alive? She has been a democratic
State, standing for freedom in self-defence among her mountains,
and in thought, in spite of race, largely on our side.

'I was astonished at U.J.'s [Stalin's] savageness against her,
and, much though I respect that great and good man, I was entirely uninfluenced by his attitude. He called them 'swine', and
he does not use that sort of language without meaning it. I am
sure we ought to stand by Switzerland, and we ought to explain
to U.J. why it is we do so. The moment for sending such a message should be carefully chosen. . . . .'

                                                    'W.S.C.'

THERE was a tense atmosphere in the Olympic stadium just
before the ceremonial march past of the teams competing in the
1936 Winter Olympic Games. I had done my best to ensure that
the members of our ski team knew the difference between the
Olympic salute, arm extended to the side, and the Nazi salute,
arm extended in front. There were rumours that some of the
teams would not salute Hitler. The competitors who received
the most rapturous welcome were those of the Austrians who
gave the Nazi salute, turning towards Hitler to make it clear that
it was the Nazi and not the Olympic salute. My own careful
instructions were wasted, for the broadcaster informed the
crowd that the 'British greet the Führer with the German salute'.
The Swiss provided an unpleasant surprise for the crowd. The

Swiss competitors in the military race were in uniform, and these saluted. Then came the civilian competitors. A momentary hesitation, and then suddenly, the Swiss ranks stiffened, and the descendants of the men who fought for freedom at Morgarten walked past Hitler eyes to the front, arms stiffly to the side.

No cheers from the crowd.

No comments from the broadcaster.

I looked back to the balcony on which Hitler was standing. His face was distorted with venomous hatred. 'God help the Swiss,' I thought, 'if ever Hitler invades their country.'

I remembered that moment four years later, on a day when a German invasion of Switzerland seemed imminent. I had been lecturing for the British Council in Florence, and crossed the Swiss frontier some days after Germany invaded Holland. On May 14, 1940, I watched the smoke of burning papers rising from the garden of the French Embassy in Berne. That afternoon the French military attaché remarked to his British colleague: 'We have lost the war.'

Meanwhile the Swiss were expecting to be invaded. The Germans had been massing troops along their frontier for some days and circulating rumours to the effect that they were about to invade Switzerland. Their intention may have been to deflect French troops, badly needed elsewhere, to the Franco-Swiss frontier or to invade Switzerland if they had failed to break through the extension of the Maginot Line near Sedan. But whatever may have been their intentions, the evidences of plans for an invasion were sufficiently impressive to crowd the roads from Basel and other frontier towns with the cars of civilians escaping into the interior.

On the night of May 14th, I dined in Berne with the British Minister, Sir David Kelly. His confidence in our ultimate victory, which never wavered during the darkest months of the war, helped, as I later learned, to maintain not only the morale of the British in Berne, but also of our Swiss supporters.

During the few days which I spent in Switzerland before returning to London, I was greatly encouraged by the sturdy tone of the proclamations in which General Guisan, the Commander-in-Chief of the Swiss Army, warned the population to disregard, in the event of an invasion, any statements alleged to emanate from Swiss broadcasting stations which announced a cease-fire. There would be no surrender.

There are few professional soldiers in the Swiss Army, and Henri Guisan, a Vaudois, was not one of them. In 1940, Marcel Pilet-Golaz who, like Guisan, was a Vaudois, was the President of the Swiss Confederation. In the fateful year of 1940 he was the head of the Departement Politique, and as such responsible for foreign policy. Every member of the Bundesrat (the Swiss Cabinet) is responsible for a particular department, and becomes President in rotation for one year only.

After the French collapse, Guisan began quietly to work against Pilet-Golaz's policy of appeasement. The tension between these men was aggravated by the fact that they had always disliked each other. Both men had their ardent supporters, some of whom were still engaged in re-fighting their old battles. The controversy flared up again in Switzerland after the publication of *Spying for Peace*[1] in England, and its serialization in the *Welt-woche* (Zürich). The author, Jon Kimche, is a brilliant journalist who left Switzerland at the age of twelve, and still retains a Swiss passport, though he has spent almost all his adult life in England. During the war he was the military correspondent of the *Evening Standard* and is now the editor of the *Jewish Observer*.[2]

---

[1] Weidenfeld and Nicolson.

[2] Had M. Kimche stayed long enough in Switzerland to receive a sound education in Swiss history he would have avoided many irritating inaccuracies. He would not have referred to the Swiss Confederation as the Swiss Republic or described the British Legation in the First World War as an Embassy, for he would have known why France alone had an Embassy until recently, an anomaly which can be traced back to the days when Cantonal regiments were raised in Switzerland to fight for the King of France. (I have often wondered whether it is because the Swiss felt it inconsistent with Swiss neutrality for their one Ambassador, the French, to be the perpetual doyen of the Diplomatic Corps that they accepted a Nuncio who is *ex officio* the doyen. The Vatican is represented by an Internuncio in countries whose governments are not prepared to concede automatic precedence to the representative of the Vatican.)

Again the statement on page 75 that the Swiss 'did nothing when the French armies entered Switzerland in 1798' could never have been made by a Swiss who had been educated in Switzerland, for every Swiss has heard of the heroic resistance in Schwyz under von Reding, the hero of a sonnet by Wordsworth, of the massacre at Stans and of the battles in the Valais. Incidentally, Napoleon, who is credited by M. Kimche with disputing the Alpine passes with Suvorof, was at the time making his way back from Egypt to France.

It is incorrect that General Guisan 'could speak virtually no German'. I interviewed him for *The Times* at the end of the war, and we spoke in German because my German is more fluent than my French. It is misleading to write

# The Swiss and Their Mountains

Guisan's first problem was the control of the thousands of Germans living in Switzerland who were, as he knew, organized for subversive activities and who were working in active co-operation with a small group of Swiss Nazis, of whom fifteen were executed and many more sentenced to long terms of imprisonment. Even more serious than the problem of German espionage was the possibility that Swiss morale might crack after France fell.

In the First World War Switzerland was never in any serious danger of invasion, and if the Germans had invaded, French and Italian armies would have immediately linked up with the Swiss; but in the Second World War Italy was not an enemy, but an ally of Germany and, after the fall of France, Switzerland was entirely surrounded by the Axis Powers and economically dependent on Germany for vital supplies.

Whereas the sympathies of the German-Swiss were divided in the First World War, in the Second World War, apart from a lunatic fringe of Swiss Nazis, German Switzerland was passionately anti-Nazi. In French Switzerland there was a small but

as if the General was shocked and surprised by the state of the Swiss Army and defences at the beginning of the war. For many years he had commanded an Army Corps and been intimately concerned in all questions of national defence.

The case against Pilet-Golaz, the president of the Swiss Confederation in the fateful year of 1940 is, I am told by well-informed Swiss, even stronger than as presented by M. Kimche and does not need to be buttressed by statements which are false, such as the statement that 'Pilet-Golaz stopped the Court Martial of the German saboteurs who were caught trying to blow up a Swiss military airfield during the June crisis and returned them to Germany'. Actually these saboteurs served long terms of imprisonment and were only released between December 1950 and April 1952.

In spite of irritating inaccuracies I welcome the publication of this book. So far as the English-speaking and English-reading world is concerned it matters little whether the case against Pilet-Golaz is less or more damaging than as presented by M. Kimche, for not one English reader in a hundred has ever heard of Pilet-Golaz before reading this book. What is important is that Switzerland should be given credit for a great record in the war, and that the editors of papers such as the *Neue Zürcher Zeitung*, the *National-Zeitung* of Basle and the *Weltwoche* should receive due recognition for their stubborn resistance to the appeasement of Pilet-Golaz.

Thanks to this book General Guisan may take his place with William Tell as a symbol of Swiss resistance to tyranny and, perhaps, in years to come, guides in charge of personally conducted parties, travelling by steamer on the Lake of Lucerne, will point out the historic meadow of the Rütli and recall not only the founding fathers of the Swiss Confederation but also the momentous meeting when Guisan so effectively countered the spirit of defeatism.

132

influential minority who were certainly not pro-Nazi but who were strong supporters of Pétain.

Pilet-Golaz, like Pétain, was a defeatist who believed in the inevitability of a Nazi victory. Pétain handed back to the Germans pilots who had been shot down, many of them by our own Air Force, and Pilet-Golaz allowed German pilots, who had been forced to land in Switzerland, to return to Germany, a clear breach of neutrality but less open to censure than Pétain's action, for Pilet-Golaz was a neutral whereas France had entered the war as an ally of Great Britain.

Pilet-Golaz's supporters in Switzerland maintain that he was a great patriot who made no more concessions than were necessary to prevent the Germans invading Switzerland and to persuade the Germans to provide Switzerland with coal and other vital imports. Certainly the position of Switzerland, wholly surrounded by Axis Powers, was critical and those who negotiated with the Germans on behalf of Switzerland had to concede much that a good Swiss would hate conceding.

Pilet-Golaz's critics contend that unpublished evidence of his relations with the German Ambassador in Berne, evidence which came into the possession of the British when the archives of the German Foreign Office were made available to the victors, prove that he went to extreme lengths in his efforts to appease the Germans. It was certainly an unfortunate coincidence that on the very day (June 25, 1940) when Pétain broadcast from Bordeaux his message of surrender to the French nation, Pilet-Golaz should also have broadcast to the Swiss a message of appeasement, in which certain phrases bore an ominous resemblance to the ideology of Pétain as, for instance: 'The time for an inner renewal has come. We must look forward, determined to use our modest but useful strength in the reconstruction of the world in its state of upheaval.'

Guisan was determined that appeasement had to be defeated and the Swiss inspired with a determination never to surrender, however apparently hopeless the immediate situation. He therefore summoned all commanders, down to battalion commanders, to meet him on the historic meadow of the Rütli, by the lake of Lucerne, where the founding fathers of the Swiss Confederation had met on August 1, 1291.

The theme of the General's address was that the existence of

Switzerland was at stake and that it was their duty to counteract the propaganda of defeatists and weaklings in their own ranks, and to preach to their troops the duty of uncompromising resistance.

In later years, Guisan explained his choice of the Rütli in simple words: '*Il me fallait une terre inspiratrice. Je ne pouvais faire ça dans une salle de gymnastique.*'

Throughout the years which followed, Guisan had the country with him. There were, of course, a few Nazis. 'Two men in my company,' an artillery major remarked to me, 'were known to be Nazis. They would have been shot the moment the Germans invaded.' There was also a group which was not in the least pro-Nazi but which would have liked to muzzle the more aggressively anti-Nazi Press. Two hundred citizens, in fact, signed a petition to the Government on November 15, 1940, urging the dismissal of the more courageous and outspoken editors. To describe, as Mr Kimche does, these signatories as 'prominent Swiss citizens' is an exaggeration. I have the names of the signatories and their occupations in front of me as I write, for the Government released to the Press the names of the 'two hundred', and these were published in the *Neue Zürcher Zeitung* of January 22, 1946. There were very few prominent people among the signatories. Most of them were small innkeepers, obscure journalists, small farmers, etc.

In the Swiss Army the leading appeaser was Colonel Wille, the son of General Wille who commanded the Swiss Army during the First World War. General Wille had married a Bismarck, and his son was therefore half German. On November 7, 1934, the Social Democrats demanded in the Nationalrat that Colonel Wille should be retired because of his close relations with the Nazis (*Volksrecht*, April 27, 1961). Colonel Wille never enjoyed the confidence of General Guisan. He was never given an active service command, but was relegated to the command of infantry training.

At the end of the war the British Foreign Office brought to the attention of the Bundesrat certain German documents which had come into their possession, among them a report by the German Minister in Berne, Dr Köcher, on a conversation which he had had with Colonel Wille on October 1, 1940. During their invasion of France the German Army obtained possession of documents relating to conversations between French and Swiss officers for co-operation in the event of a German invasion of Switzerland. Wille, according to Dr Köcher, suggested that he should take up the matter of this allegedly unneutral behaviour with the Bundesrat and insist on Guisan's dismissal. These documents came to the attention of the Bundesrat in 1952. They consulted the Chef des Justiz und Polizeidepartements, who replied that no action could be taken in view of the Swiss equivalent of the statute of limitations. They sent for Colonel Wille, who flatly denied that he had made any such suggestions, and who insisted that Köcher was concerned to emphasize his importance to the Germans and thus to prevent his recall. In 1959 Wille died, and when the German documents were published early in 1961 the Bundesrat distributed a memorandum in which they maintained that it was impossible to arrive at any certain conclusions, but it was improbable that Köcher had invented the conversation though he may have had a tendency to write in such a way as to improve his own position. What was certainly true was that there existed great differences of opinion between Guisan and Wille, and that Wille was the advocate of demobilization. Wille's relations with the Minister must be condemned even if he believed himself to be acting in the interests of his country. Had these facts been disclosed in time, it would have been necessary to open an investigation. (*Neue Zürcher Zeitung* April 25, 1961.)

From all I hear, Wille and his small clique had not the slightest influence in the army or in the country.

The creation of the Réduit, the mountain redoubt into which the Swiss Army would have retreated in the event of an invasion, was not completed for at least eighteen months after the Rütli speech, but even in 1940 preparations for the 'scorched earth' policy were far advanced, and many of the factories which were producing munitions and precision tools for the Germans would have been destroyed even at that comparatively early stage of the war. Even more important was the fact that both the Gotthard and the Simplon tunnels, so essential for the communications between Germany and Italy, would have been put out of action the moment that the German invasion started. Finally, the Germans did not underestimate the stubborn courage of the Swiss soldier defending his homeland.

A Swiss friend of mine, Herr Werner Grob, who had served under General Guisan, and who was old enough to remember the First World War in which the Swiss Army was commanded by General Wille, drew an interesting comparison between the two generals. 'Wille,' he said, 'had married a Bismarck, and his military outlook was influenced by his admiration for the German Army. He wasn't popular with the rank and file of our Army. Guisan, on the other hand, though he understood the supreme importance of discipline, was a real father to his men. He inspired not only great respect but great affection. When France fell we were surrounded by Germany and Italy and there were not a few who felt that it would be useless to resist an invasion. In that critical hour Guisan was to Switzerland what Churchill was to your country. He made us all feel that it was far, far better to go down fighting than to surrender.'

Guisan died fifteen years later and was buried in Lausanne on April 12, 1960. 'The world outside,' writes Mr Kimche, 'if it had ever heard of General Guisan, had long forgotten him. But in the Swiss homes, without orders or instructions, without designation, over two hundred thousand former soldiers of the General donned their full dress uniforms, put on their black bands of mourning, and travelled to Lausanne at their own expense to pay a last tribute such as was given to no other war commander anywhere. For these two hundred thousand Swiss knew what they—and the world—owed to Henri Guisan, their General.'

No attempt to estimate the nature and extent of the influence of the mountains on the Swiss would be complete which omitted all reference to the Second World War, and to the effect of the mountain Réduit on Swiss morale. 'The fact that we could retire into the Réduit,' a Swiss remarked to me, 'and hold out perhaps for years, was all important for our morale.' In those dark days and difficult years many a Swiss lifted up his eyes to the hills and found the help he needed to continue the struggle.

# 14

## THE INFLUENCE OF THE TOURIST
## ON THE BERGLER

MY FIRST clear memory as a child is of the great fire which, in the summer of 1892, consumed most of the village of Grindelwald and of the chalet in which we were then living. The Anglican church was burnt, but the Zwinglian church, to which we were often taken as children, escaped the flames. In those days, the dominant personality of the village was not a leading hotelier but the village Pfarrer, Dr Strasser, a tall, powerfully built man with a voice that filled every cranny of the church. He was not only a fine preacher but a mountaineer. The *Gletcher-Pfarrer*, as he was affectionately called, was a great friend of Andreas Fischer, a remarkable guide who took a Doctorate of Letters and ultimately gave up guiding for a post in the University of Basel. He perished in a snowstorm on the Aletschhorn. Fischer was a sceptic, and an admirer of Schopenhauer. 'Schopenhauer,' wrote Strasser to his friend, 'is the most dangerous, most brilliant, most original and most clear-cut betrayer of the heavenly state. A true Oberländer and glacier man cannot be a follower of Schopenhauer.'

Strasser's church was always full, and this in spite of the fact that many of his congregation spent the summer in the cattle alps of Grindel, Buss or Scheidegg, and had to trudge back for two or three hours after the service. Strasser did what he could to protect the traditional way of life of the Berglers, and watched with anxiety the influence of the tourists on that life. This indeed was the theme of many of his sermons. My mother, as the wife of a travel agent, shared his anxieties, and sometimes quoted Strasser's remarks on this subject to my father.

My mother was a good linguist, spoke German fluently and understood the Bernese dialect. She made many real friendships with the villagers, among them a boy to whom she gave occasional lessons in English, and who was destined to become the first

Socialist President of the Swiss Confederation, Bundesrat Ernst Nobs. We dined together a few weeks after the Second World War had ended. He spoke to me with great affection of my mother, and was not surprised when I told him that, thanks to her, even as a child I realized that it was not the main function of the Swiss to provide hotels for the tourists and guides for mountaineers.

Bundesrat Nobs was a Socialist, but a Socialist with a difference, for Marxism has no appeal to the true Bergler. Nobs had known Lenin living as an exile in Switzerland. 'I once asked Lenin,' he said to my son Peter, 'in which country he thought that the revolution would break out first. Lenin said, "In Switzerland, because in your country every citizen keeps his rifle at home, so you start with the great advantage of an armed proletariat. You must then begin by creating a cell of ten revolutionaries whom you can implicitly trust, and each of them will then create a similar cell of ten. Begin in Zürich, and when you have got ten thousand revolutionaries, give the word. Tell them to take their rifles and shoot the town councillors and take possession of the town." "If we were to give these instructions to the workers," Nobs replied, "they would say, '*Dazu ist das Gewehr nicht da*' (That is not what the rifle is for)." '

## Guides and Amateurs

Ruskin's Swiss friends, he tells us, 'spoke with chief fear of the influx of English wealth, gradually connecting all industry with the wants and ways of strangers, and inviting all idleness to depend upon their casual help; thus gradually resolving the ancient consistency and pastoral simplicity of the mountain life into the two irregular trades of innkeepers and mendicants'.[1]

Though many of Pfarrer Strasser's sermons were on some such theme as this, the *Gletscher Pfarrer* would have been the first to make an exception for the influence of the real mountaineer on the Bergler who accompanied him as a guide. In the course of this book I have quoted tributes paid by Captain J. P. Farrar to two great guides, Daniel Maquinaz and Christian Klucker, tributes to the quality of mountain friendship between guide and amateur which would be endorsed by any amateur lucky enough to have climbed with an outstanding guide.

[1] *Modern Painters* iv, 20, 40.

A vivid portrait of Joseph Knubel emerges from the pages of Geoffrey Young's book, *On High Hills*. No guide of that period had a finer record for first ascents in summer, or a longer list of pioneer ski tours, than Knubel. I have only once climbed with Knubel in summer, but he was my guide on innumerable glacier ski tours. Unlike many guides who are content to earn their money as easily as possible by leading parties on hackneyed glacier tours, Lötschenlücke, Galmilücke, etc, J.K. had an amateur's interest in pioneering on ski, and a real pride in carrying through such eccentric tours as the traverse with ski of the Trifthorn from the Mountet Hut to Zermatt. We followed the long arrête from the Trifthorn to a point near the Triftjoch, our ski tied together and lowered from ledge to ledge. 'I tell you, Mr Lunn,' said J.K. when we reached the glacier in safety, 'not one guide will repeat this tour with ski.' Another ski tour which we both enjoyed and which has not, I think, been repeated, was from the Weisshorn Hut (after climbing the Weisshorn) across a shoulder of the Weisshorn to the Biesjoch and then to the Turtmanntal.

'Knubel,' writes Geoffrey Young, 'was as reserved and aloof as a forest Indian, with a primitive head, thin bleached hair and the eyes of a dreamer.' His position in the hierarchy of guides was not solely determined by his mountaineering achievements, but also by his shy aloofness and reluctance to take the position which would gladly have been conceded to him by his peers. His dress was quietly distinctive. Even after a long climb he still looked soigné. He was sometimes uneasily aware of the contrast, in this respect, between his appearance and mine. I remember a four-day ski tour among the glaciers, nearly fifty years ago, which ended at Zermatt. Zermatt in those days had no winter season, and the valley had hardly seen a tourist for six months. A thousand feet above Zermatt, Knubel produced a pocket comb and a pocket mirror and, after completing his toilette, looked me over with a rather worried expression. He hinted that I might like to put on a collar. I rummaged in my sack and extracted a detachable soft collar, which Knubel examined thoughtfully. He pulled some string out of his pocket, took the exact measurement of my neck, and darted off down to the valley. He was waiting for me at the entrance of the village with a new collar of the latest Zermatt cut.

Knubel always spoke with a most moving affection of 'Herr Young', and seemed indifferent to his own reputation. His was a simplicity which might almost be described as *sancta simplicitas*. He knew nothing of the life of the city, and his rare contact with the great world bewildered and sometimes alarmed him. He once spent a few hours in Geneva, and described to me in tones of shocked dismay how a woman, whom he could not remember ever to have met, stopped him in the street. He wondered what she wanted. 'You will hardly believe, Herr Lunn, but she wanted me to go back with her to her rooms.' I registered the right reaction to this tale of unprecedented vice.

J.K. was one of the guests of honour at a luncheon party at the Riffelalp when Zermatt was celebrating the centenary of the first ascent of Monte Rosa. Graceful references to J.K. were made by the chairman, and Knubel, to his obvious discomfort, realized that he had to reply. His speech was very short. 'I always said my prayers before a climb and tried to do my duty.'

Knubel died a few months after another dear companion in the mountains, Fritz Amacher. Knubel was famous, Amacher obscure. He was the boots at the Pension Wolter when we first met and the boots at the Hotel Adler when I last saw him.

In the course of an article describing a ski tour in the Oberland glaciers in 1923, Lord Dowding made some amusing comments on Fritz and his brother Adolf (who died some years before Fritz).

'The Amachers compensated for their laziness in the huts by their amazing energy as weight carriers. The ultimate straw which shall break the backs of Fritz and Adolf Amacher is yet to find, and they sauntered along with the utmost nonchalance under heavy burdens, grievous to be borne. Fritz was the possessor of an imperfectly suppressed sense of humour, wasted on (and indeed misplaced) in a porter. . . . Fritz relieved the tedium of the journey by describing with saturnine humour a three-year-old expedition during which he, Lunn and two other unfortunates subsisted for two days on no other substance than toffee caramels, and a chunk of weevily bread found under the stove in the Dollfuss Hut.'

Fritz's ironic sense of humour was often in evidence. I remember when we were wriggling up a crack in a vertical wall of ice, on the first ski ascent of the Eiger, Fritz remarking that he was so glad we had carried our ski through the ice-fall as it would be such fun carrying them down again. We had no guide and it is against the rules for a porter to accompany a guideless party, and Fritz was tackled by the guides on his return from the Eiger. 'I just told them,' he said to me, 'that if I like to carry ski for my old friend Lunn, that's no business of anybody else.'

Dowding's tribute to his weight-carrying powers was more than deserved. He was absolutely untiring. At the end of 1919 he and I had the most wonderful week of ski-ing on lesser mountains that I have ever enjoyed. I was at Grindelwald at the time and the Wengenalp railway was not running.

On the Monday we climbed from Grund to the Scheidegg (3,660 feet ascent). On Tuesday from Grund to the Lauberhorn (5,020 feet ascent). On Wednesday we climbed the Schwarzhorn (6,144 feet ascent). On Thursday the Wildgerst (6,019 feet ascent, 7,488 feet descent) and, after a day's rest, traversed the Faulhorn to Meiringen by the long route via Sägisalp (about 8,000 feet of climbing and about 9,500 feet of downhill ski-ing). Neither of us had done the run before, but though we struck a mist at 5,000 feet we never missed the best line. This is one of the most enchanting ski-runs in the Alps. During these five tours we averaged just under 5,800 feet of climbing per day and in every case we started by a climb up a path with Fritz carrying two pairs of ski, foot-climbs which varied from about 1,500 to 2,000 feet. Another exacting test of his strength was the tour of the Wetterhörner, when we did the four Wetterhorn passes, Wetter-Limmi, Rose-negg, back via Mitteljoch to the Wetterkessel and up again to the Wettersattel, and then climbed two peaks of the Wetterhorn, Hasli Jungfrau and Mittelhorn, and traversed the Renfenhorn on our return to the Gauli. We climbed 8,000 feet that day, and were detained next day in the Gauli by *foehn,* ran out of provisions and crossed the Hühnerthäli Pass and Finsteraarhorn to the Strahlegg on 'toffee caramels and a chunk of weevily bread'. Knubel was our guide and 'Schluny', for fifty years concierge of the Palace, Mürren, had joined us in an amateur capacity.

Fritz was with me on many other expeditions, amongst them the first crossing of the Galmilücke on ski.

He was a perfect companion not only because he could always extract a wry chuckle out of unpleasant situations, but also because he loved not only the 'chief things of the ancient mountains', but also the little things. I remember on a March run as we approached the valley we passed a steep southern slope which had just discarded its last moist rags of snow. A rash little crocus had thrust itself through the young grass. Fritz sniffed the spring in the air and chuckled with joy.

Our last run together was in 1938. We climbed 3,500 feet up the Chrisegg ridge, where the 'First' chair-lift now offers painless transport to the skiers.

'At the end of last season,' said Fritz, 'four visitors engaged me for a week to carry their lunches. And I would not let them be lazy. So we never took the train to the Scheidegg but spent all our time climbing up this side of the valley and we didn't ski wildly downhill like the young skiers. And at the end they were very thankful to me and I told them that it was you who had taught me when I was a boy to like this nice Touren-Skifahren. The way you and I ski gives us time to look round and see something of the mountains and not only the tips of our ski.'

I shall not forget the golden hour we spent above Grindelalp, 'the still unravished bride of loveliness', the silence unbroken by the sound of the chair-lift, as yet unbuilt. It was, though we did not know it, the last of many such quiet mountain hours which we spent together. The great peaks across the valley were haunted by shared memories of great adventure. Fritz pointed with a cheerful chuckle to the Berglistock. 'We were much less pleased,' he said, 'to get to the top than to get to the bottom.' He was right. We reached the summit far too late on a May afternoon and on the descent were forced to cross and re-cross the gullies which seam the face, gullies swept intermittently by wet snow avalanches. We were lucky, for we scampered across the broadest of the gullies before an avalanche fell, and a little lower I was just beginning to pay out the rope while Fritz advanced when, once again, the snow flooded down the gully we were about to enter.

On our descent from Grindelalp we were joined by a solitary skier whom we had seen just above as we rested. Skiers may be divided into two great groups, those who own sealskins and those who do not. And the man who owns sealskins I am ready to meet as a friend, for though we may differ on all else, at least mountains for us are not merely things down which you slide. Our unknown friend told us that he was employed by a famous ski shop in Berne and added, with a reproachful glance at the Scheidegg slopes, '*Die Leute sind verrückt. Sie fahren wild hinunter. Die Ski gehen kaputt, Die Stöcke gehen kaputt, Die Kanten gehen kaputt. Gut für's Geschäft. Immerhin verkaufe ich lieber Seehundsfelle.*'[1]

Fritz nodded his agreement.

A year later the war broke out and Fritz and I never skied again together, but I never went to Grindelwald without looking him up. He liked mountains in the way I like them, and we did not need the mechanism of consecutive conversation to revive our common memories. An incomplete allusion to some shared experience, or the echo of an old joke, served 'to beget the golden time again'.

Fritz never married, and in the hierarchy of the hotel world he did not rise very high. It was among the mountains and only among the mountains that he found that romance without which life is drab indeed.

A year or two before he died, Scott Lindsay and I were strolling through Grindelwald when suddenly we met Fritz. 'I want to introduce a friend of mine,' I said to Scott. 'Not "a friend",' said Fritz reproachfully, 'but rather one of his oldest and best friends.'

*The Influence of Winter Sports on the Bergler*
What is the influence of winter sports on the Bergler? My Swiss friends look thoughtful when I ask them this question, for that influence, as they all agree, has been partly beneficial and partly mischievous. Winter sports, by creating a second tourist season in the year, have greatly increased the Bergler's chances of making money and thus checked the flight from the mountains to the towns. This fact alone is admitted to tilt the balance decisively in favour of winter sports. But, of course, the influence is not wholly beneficial. The Bergler, who sees the tourist in holiday mood, does not always understand that there is a great contrast between the winter sportsman on holiday, with his hour at the bar before and after dinner, and the winter sportsman at home, and is in danger of regarding this holiday life as the norm to

[1] 'People are mad. They ski madly downhill. The ski break, the edges crack, the sticks break. It's good for business, but I'd rather sell sealskins.'

which he too should aspire. Drink is a problem in mountain valleys as elsewhere, and a generous employer who is always standing a favourite ski-teacher a drink may encourage him to develop expensive habits which he cannot afford.

Again, the *character* of the winter clientèle has not changed for the better since the early days of winter sports.

'Certainly,' a Swiss friend of mine writes, 'the relations between the Berglers and their British guests are not what they were before 1914. The main reason for this is that far more English visit us today than then. Among these great masses are many Britons who behave in "unBritish" ways, with the result that the respect for their nation declines. It is no less certain that in our region the English are by and large regarded as very welcome guests. And this not only for the money which they spend, but also our relations with them were in general very pleasant and because we appreciated their outlook and sporting code. We all have many good friends among the British and welcome the chance to see them again among us.'

A characteristic of the age in which we live is the criticism of accepted standards and the revolt against form, the form which, whether in life or in art, is the product of discipline. It would be surprising if the relations between skiers and ski-ing guides had been wholly uninfluenced by the relaxing of standards, and it is evidence of the strength of traditional codes that the majority of those who guide skiers on the glaciers have as keen a sense of their responsibilities as the men who, in the nineteenth century, created the great tradition of the Alpine guides. There are, of course, some exceptions such as the guides whose conduct was criticized in the editorial of the *Downhill Only Club Journal*, 1959, from which the following candid criticisms are quoted:

'A competent ski-instructor is not necessarily equipped with the professional qualifications of the Kalbermattens or the Knubels, Anereggs or Lochmatters of yesteryear. Nor have they acquired a knowledge and understanding of the correct relationship between guides and employer, which was so rigidly maintained and fostered by their forefathers. You do not, today, expect your Alpine guide to unlace your boots at the end of a hard day's work, but a client has the right to expect a minimum standard of service in the huts. Such chores as lighting fires, cooking, washing

24  FERDINAND HODLER (1853–1918). Breithorn 1911. Oil. (Art Museum, Lucerne)

up, airing blankets, however, are often left to the hut warden or
to the client himself.

'The same sort of thing is apt to arise on the Lötschenlücke any
sunny day in March. After a two-hour climb a newcomer to the
glaciers may arrive at the col stiff and tired, only to find the so-
called guide a black speck on the glacier below, sheltering out of
the wind and encouraging his client to make haste; and little
wonder that the novice is so irritated by the guide who leads on
without helping when a skin strapping breaks, that he decides to
stick to the piste in future. Some little time ago a party of inex-
perienced tourers arrived at Blatten where their guide left them
to find their own way down to the valley (some fifteen miles of
icy path) while he disappeared through the back door of a nearby
chalet. They had no idea of the distance involved and, therefore,
how fast they should go in order to catch their train. Half the
party pushed off at high speed and soon became separated, two of
them taking a wrong turning in Wiler. The other half visited
every pub en route (which, we agree, is in the proper manner of
things) and nearly missed the train. The one girl in the party
arrived terrified and exhausted, having sustained a nasty fall and
skied down alone in the gathering darkness with a broken ski tip.
Of course, the most experienced skier amongst the party should
have been deputed to lead them down while the guide brought up
the stragglers in the rear.

'On the other hand, experienced tourers should not expect to
be completely shepherded along every step—and yet too many of
us behave like sheep, blindly following our guide without question and showing little or no interest in the problems of route
finding and mountaincraft. No wonder, then, that the modern
ski-guide rarely thinks of consulting his client as to the route or
imposing upon him more than the slightest grain of responsibility.

'But, as we mentioned before, we are the cause and the remedy
lies with us. "In the beginning we like the English. Now we
realize that they only come to our mountains to drink and to
corrupt our children"—and this is not the first time this has been
said. We spend our evenings tippling with our ski-instructors
and are on back-slapping terms with them during the day. Our
wives and sisters invest them with an aura of romance and treat
them like long-lost relatives from Australia at the beginning of

each season. In the night-clubs we see our girls flirting with the young Ski-lehrers, who are probably bored and only too anxious to get home to their wives.

'Can we now complain when all this familiarity has indeed bred much contempt? In the words of Lord Wolsey, we should "strive to be intimate without being familiar".'

The Oberland is today, as in the past, the nursery of great guides, to whose achievements a tribute has been paid in the preceding pages. The editorial in the *D.H.O. Journal* seemed to me worth quoting, less for its criticism of the exceptional deviations from that great tradition which the guides of the last century created, than for its salutary reminder that there are *some* skiers whose influence on the Bergler leaves a great deal to be desired. Fortunately there are other skiers who have helped to redress the balance. Both Berglers and amateurs who raced against each other in the Golden Age of Alpine racing were the better for the generous rivalry of a great sport.

*The Influence of Ski-racing on Anglo-Swiss Relations*
The British, as we have seen, were the pioneers of the Alpine races, Downhill and Slalom, and because they were the first to develop these races they could, though greatly outnumbered, put up a fine performance against the Berglers in the early days of Alpine racing. Our girls were at one time the best racers in Europe, and our men often won international events and were well placed in the pre-war World Championships and Olympic Games.

The annual race between the British and Swiss University Ski Clubs (first held on Janary 11 and 12, 1925) is the oldest international event decided on the combined result of a downhill and slalom race. Before this match was instituted by by Walter Amstutz and me there were hardly any contacts between British and Swiss undergraduates. Till then the British met the Swiss in various roles, as genial and popular hotel proprietors, as guides and as ski-teachers, but they seldom met the Swiss who had no business connected with the tourist traffic. And such Swiss start with a bias against foreigners who treat their country as a mere 'playground of Europe', to quote the infelicitous title of a delightful Alpine classic. The Anglo-Swiss races broke down many barriers and established the friendliest of relations between the university skiers of the two countries. There was a moment when the British were actually leading in the series but, of course, the odds against us are very great and we are now quite content to win, as we do, about one such match out of five.

Before the Second World War, our best racers occasionally won international races which were not restricted to university students. Now whereas the great triumphs of our mountaineers had been for the most part achieved with the help of Swiss guides, the ski-ing victories which we recall with the greatest pride were achieved in competition with the best of the Swiss Berglers. Among the great racers of those days were men who evoked in the Swiss not only respect but affection. To name only those who are no longer with us, the deaths of Antony Knebworth and Dick Waghorn before the war, and of Jimmy Palmer-Tomkinson after the war, were hardly less mourned by Swiss racers than by us. Knebworth and Waghorn, winner of the Schneider Trophy, were killed flying, Palmer-Tomkinson while practising for the British Ski Championship in 1952.

And those of us who remember the beginnings of Alpine racing recall with great affection the outstanding personalities of some of the leading Swiss racers of those days, Otto Furrer, for instance, who was killed on the Matterhorn, and David Zogg of Arosa, both great personalities as well as great skiers.

The value which the British racers attached to their relations with Swiss skiers was demonstrated when the Olympic Committee announced on the eve of the 1936 Winter Olympic Games that ski-teachers were not eligible. Now, of course, we were not prepared to defend the rule of the International Ski Federation, under which a ski-teacher was regarded as an amateur. Our point was that the whole amateur façade of the Olympic Games was ridiculous, and that the Swiss ski-teachers had, if anything, a better claim to be considered amateurs than a rival team who had started their training on the glaciers in August and were obviously receiving broken-time payment, which was also against Olympic rules.

The Swiss, French and Austrians agreed to boycott the Alpine races in the Olympic Games, and they asked for and obtained our support. Our racers were ready to sacrifice the fun of competing in the Olympic Games because of their ties of friendship with the

Swiss. In my long experience of international sport, I can recall countless cases of teams protesting against decisions which robbed them of victory or which reduced their chances of victory. The British protest at the 1936 Olympic Games is the only case I know of a team protesting against a decision which improved their chances, for we had no ski-teachers in our team and our most dangerous rivals were ski-teachers. Eventually the proposed boycott broke down because the French Government had been subsidizing ski-racing on the understanding that France would enter teams for all the ski events at Garmisch.

# 15

## THE MOUNTAIN WAY OF LIFE

SWITZERLAND is today an independent country mainly because the Habsburgs found it far more difficult to bring pressure on their subjects in the Alpine valleys than on their subjects in the plains. The mountains foster among mountain dwellers a spirit of independence. The fathers of the Swiss Confederation were men of the mountains who instinctively resisted the attempt to govern them from the plains. They did not willingly accept any authority other than the authority of those whom they themselves had chosen to administer their own affairs. The story of William Tell enshrines the race memories of a collective rather than of an individual attitude. The Landvogt Gessler, whom Tell slew, was hated not because he was an Austrian, for the founders of Switzerland were not nationalists as that term is now understood, but because he had been appointed by the Habsburgs to impose Habsburg government on the stubborn men of the mountains. The spirit which created Swiss independence still survives in the mountains of Switzerland. In the fourth year of the Second World War a local paper in the Grisons reported the indignant protest of a mountain peasant against the necessary controls which the Government could not avoid imposing. 'How can one speak,' he exclaimed, 'of freedom when one can't even fatten a calf without a special permit or sell a little bit of land without permission from the State? What is the use of such regulations. The Landvogt Gessler said, "I won't allow peasants to build houses without my permission." '

The word 'democracy', which is perverted by the Communists, their so-called 'popular democracies' being neither democracies nor popular, is far from being a precise term even in the free world. A more exact classification of democracies is indeed long overdue. Even in a small country such as Switzerland there are not only differences in the democratic governments of the different Cantons which are recognized officially in the words employed to differentiate, for instance, the Landesgemeinde from other forms of democratic government, but also differences of attitude as yet undefined in actual terms, the difference, for instance, between what I suggest might be described as personal and impersonal democracies.

The Landesgemeinde, which still function in the mountain Cantons of Glarus, Appenzell and Unterwalden, are assemblies in which every adult citizen meets and approves or rejects laws submitted to the entire adult citizenship of the Canton. This is indeed government of the people by the people for the people, and not government of the people by a political party mainly for the supporters of that party. 'Where the entire people,' writes Dr Richard Weiss in his fascinating book, *Volkskunde der Schweiz*, 'stands shoulder to shoulder, and almost every man knows every other member of the community, where the administration is from man to man rather than from office to office, from mouth to mouth and not from paper to paper, as it still is in the Landesgemeinde Cantons of Glarus, Appenzell and Unterwalden, there is still a close contact between Home and State. There one still says "Land" when one means State and Home.'[1]

This mountain democracy of the Berglers, as the mountain men describe themselves, is not a manufactured constitution imposed from above, like the democratic constitutions imposed on India and Nigeria in imitation of the West. It is an organic democracy which has evolved naturally and has its popular roots in local government in the various Gemeinde which are responsible for local affairs, such as the Kirchgemeinde and Schulgemeinde. Patriotism begins, as Burke somewhere says, with our feeling for 'the little platoon' of which we are a member. The contrast between what I have called personal as opposed to impersonal democracy is reflected in the Berglers' attitude to the State. Whereas the urban proletariat seek to change the State and transform it from a bourgois-capitalistic into a Socialist or Marxist State, the peasant dislikes the State as such. The very word State did not exist in the old folk language. To the Bergler the word suggests taxes, innumerable forms to fill up, and the modern successors of the old Bailiffs, the Habsburg Vögte. As a

[1] *Volkskunde der Schweiz*, published by Eugen Rentsch Verlag Erlenbach, p. 334.

result, there has always been a cleavage between the laws imposed by the State and the customs and ethical codes which have evolved organically in the community. Hence the popular saying that *Orstbrauch* is superior to *Landrecht*.

Newman's contrast between 'real assent' and 'notional assent' could be illustrated by the contrast between the notional assent which the Bergler gives to what the law enjoins and his real assent to the code of the community. A Bergler who lived in one of the valleys of the Bündner Oberland, whose southern mountains divide Switzerland from Italy, was convicted of smuggling. His righteous indignation was passionate in its sincerity. He explained that he had no other profession and that he had been a smuggler since the age of sixteen and had a wife and children to support. He might have committed an offence against *Landrecht* but he had acted in accordance with *Ortsbrauch*.

'Those who,' to quote Burke once again, 'are so preoccupied with the rights of man that they have totally forgotten his nature,' tend to equate democracy with egalitarianism. Democracy is only egalitarian in so far as elections are decided by the egalitarian principle of one man one vote, but man is a hierarchical animal and snobbery is the key to evolution, for if our ape-like ancestors had been less anxious to climb the social ladder, we should still be climbing trees.

In Switzerland, as elsewhere, the egalitarianism of the sinner which is inspired by resentment or superiority, 'I'm as good as you are', is more common than the egalitarianism of the saint which is based on humility, 'You're as good as I am', and the Berglers have always been quick to condemn any pretentions acquired by those who had mixed with the great world. In the seventeenth century the Grisons held the key to the Valtelline, the strategically important valley coveted both by the French and the Austrians. Ambassadors from the Grisons were treated with great honour at the French Court, and some of them were painted in their Ambassadorial robes, but in the family portraits which were displayed in their homes they were indistinguishable so far as clothes were concerned from their fellow citizens.

There was nothing egalitarian about the republican simplicity which would have made it impossible for one of the leading citizens of the Grisons, which was then an independent State, to hang on the walls of his own home a portrait of himself in the court dress which he wore at the Court of the French King. Nor was the official who posted the results of a ski race in which the Spanish Prince, H.R.H. Prince Alonso de Orleans-Bourbon, had competed and who described him as Bourbon, Alf, a doctrinaire apostle of egalitarianism. A mild comment of mine on 'Bourbon, Alf' elicited from another Swiss the retort, 'We Swiss are not interested in titles.' 'Why then,' I asked, 'is one of the competitors described on the result list as "Dr Roth"?' '*Das hat er verdient,*' was the reply, '*Der Prinzen titel kommt aus dem Bett.*' ('He earned the title of "Doctor", but the Prince's title came out of the bed.') 'So did the doctor's title,' I retorted. 'Brains are just as much an accident of birth as the title of Prince.' But my friend was unconvinced.

It would, however, be wrong to assume that achievement is all that counts with Berglers, and that the Bergler hierarchy ignores all '*aus dem Bett*' qualifications. In Grindelwald, those who can trace their descent from the first settlers who migrated from the Lötschental in the thirteenth century, feel themselves very much the superiors of those whose forebears emigrated from the shores of Lake Brienz and settled in the valley in the eighteenth century, and both groups refer with disdain to recent arrivals as *Zuehagaschlingget*, which may be rendered 'those who have slunk in'. In Mürren the old Mürren families will often foregather and inveigh against the fact that most of the money in Mürren goes into the pockets of the *Fetzel*, a pejorative term applied to those who are not Mürrenites by birth but who have acquired hotels or shops in Mürren.

In many mountain valleys the Burgers constitute an oligarchy based on birth. Every Bergler has the right to vote in elections for the Gemeinde which is responsible for the affairs of the community, but you do not acquire merely by residence any right to join the Burgerschaft, which is often a considerable property owner. In Zermatt, for instance, the Burgerschaft not only owns the grazing rights of the cattle alps but also two hotels, the hotel on the Riffelberg and the Zermatterhof in Zermatt.

Zermatt was created as a tourist centre by Alexander Seiler, who was a Burger of the little village of Blitzingen in the Upper Rhone Valley. His application to become a Burger of Zermatt was refused. Though a Valaisian, and though the Burger of a village less than a hundred miles from Zermatt, he was still regarded as a quasi-foreigner. He appealed to the Canton of Valais, who fixed a sum which he would be required to pay to become a Burger, and insisted that he be admitted. The Burgers appealed to the Nationalrat in Berne (one of the two houses of Parliament) and when they supported the Canton, the Burgerschaft appealed to the Bundesrat (the Cabinet), the Bundesversammlung (both houses of Parliament) and finally to the Federal Court of Appeal in Lausanne, which confirmed the findings of the Bundesrat, Nationalrat and Cantonal Government. But it was not until the Swiss Government sent a platoon of soldiers to Zermatt that the Burgers gave in. That was on April 7, 1889, but the main fight did not end with the admission of the Seilers. When the Gornergrat railway was built, the Burgers were delighted that the railway passed conveniently close to the Riffelberg Hotel, which they owned, but was separated from the Riffelalp Hotel, owned by the Seilers, by land which the Burgers owned. The Seilers opened negotiations to buy the necessary land to build a little road from the Riffelalp station to their hotel, but the Burgers refused to sell. The Seilers thereupon asked the Federal Government for a concession to build a *railway* from the Riffelalp station to their hotel. This concession was granted. The necessary land for the railway was expropriated by the Federal Government, and the little electric tram which transports luggage from the station to the hotel is, in theory, the railway for which the Seilers obtained the concession.

Now, as I have said, Alexander Seiler belonged to the same Canton as the Zermatter Burgers, but he might as well have been a foreigner. I remember once reminding the organizer of a race in a famous Oberland centre that according to one of the international rules, for which I was in fact responsible, the referee had to be a foreigner. 'But we did appoint a foreigner,' exclaimed my friend. In this case the 'foreigner' came from Berne.

Some of the fiercest mountain feuds are not between valley and valley but between parties in the same mountain village. Nothing could be more misleading than the widely held conception of the Swiss as rather dull, worthy, law-abiding democrats, the conception which finds expression in the remark of one of the characters in Graham Greene's *The Third Man*, 'The Swiss have had five centuries of peace and democracy and what have they produced? The cuckoo clock.' During these five centuries of alleged peace, Switzerland has been the scene of three civil wars and seven wars against foreign powers. Prior to the nineteenth century Switzerland was not a democracy but a federation of quasi-sovereign cantons, some of which were democratic, some of which were governed by oligarchies and some of which were subject cantons, Vaud, for instance, which was governed by Berne. Finally, though cuckoo clocks are now made in Switzerland, they originated in the Black Forest, and the Swiss who are rightly proud of their watch industry much resent being credited with the paternity of the cuckoo clock.

A great charm of Switzerland is its cultural variety. There are, of course, many Swiss who conform to the popular conception of worthy law-abiding democrats, but this particular type was not over-represented among those citizens of Saxon who supply the Swiss market with fruit, and who resented the climatic injustice which enables Italian fruit to ripen earlier and reach the Swiss market before the fruit grown in Switzerland. Their protest took the form of burning a freight train full of Italian fruit on its way through Saxon.

There are mountain valleys in which local politics evoke passions and violence reminiscent of city feuds in Rennaissance Italy. There is a certain village, which I do not propose to name, in a canton which I prefer not to indicate, the report of whose elections in a local paper circulating through that region ended with the words, 'We are glad to report that nobody was killed during the elections,' but this reassuring statement was followed in the Stop Press news column with the statement, 'We regret to report that there was one fatal casualty of which we were unaware when we wrote our report, but only one, which is an improvement on last year.'

The elections are important because of the spoils system. The party in power have a certain amount of patronage to dispose of. There are mountain villages where 40 per cent of the population belong to one family clan, and another 40 per cent to another family clan. Each clan has its own candidates for every post, and is own local *Wirtschaft*. Even the cows are sometimes made to feel the results of the collective vendetta.

Mountain valleys are, of course, feeling the effects of the wind of change which sweeps up from the towns and plains. In the Inner Oberland, many of the Berglers, including most of those who work on railways, were captured for the Socialist Party by two brilliant schoolmasters, but the Bergler Socialist is very different from the urban Socialist. The Bergler is never a Marxist.

Moreover, even in those mountain valleys where the two-clan system still prevails, the multiple-party system is gradually being adopted, even though it is often the target for mockery by those who feel that the traditional two-party feud is ideal. Dr Weiss quotes in this connection the uninhibited comment on the multiparty system in an open discussion by a Prätigauer peasant:

'*Früher heds nu zwäi Partyä ggee: di Liberalä und die Konservativä, und duo isch's guät ggangä. Hüt hets ä ganze Tschuppä Partyä: aber mee as zwäi Tütti hed d'Muätär Helvetia halt nid- I han gschlossä.*' I am no expert on Swiss dialects, but the sense of the above seems to me clear: 'Formerly there were only two parties, the Liberals and the Conservatives, and for that reason it worked well. Now there is a whole lot of parties, but Mother Helvetia has not more than two breasts. I have finished.'

*The Influence of Mountains in preserving Local Cultures*
The Far West Kandahar had just been successfully completed in the Yosemite, and the cup itself, presented by the Kandahar Ski Club, had been won by a Swiss, Martin Fopp of Davos. He had spent only a few weeks in America and he was suffering from an acute attack of homesickness.

'In Switzerland,' he said, 'you travel a few hours and the language changes and the customs change. *Das hat einen Reiz* (that has a charm). But here you travel six thousand kilometres from New York to San Francisco and you find the same newspaper and the same food and the same people as when you started.'

If he had known America better he would have appreciated the great difference between New York and San Francisco, but it is undeniable that cultural differences are tending to disappear. In the nineteenth century the Boston Brahmin, the Kentucky Colonel, the Southern Aristocrat and the Far West Pioneer were sharply differentiated types, but today radio and television and other means of mass communication are eroding regional differences. The same process is at work in Switzerland, but it meets with more resistance. The great mission of the mountains is to keep people apart, and it is the fierce sense of independence, native to mountain valleys, which preserves cultural differences. Every true Swiss can make his own the prayer, '*Mannigfaltigkeit in der Einheit, welche Gott uns erhalten möge*' (May God preserve our variety in unity).

There is indeed, as Martin Fopp truly said, a great *Reiz* in all the sharp contrast of this mountain land. You can travel in a few hours from Zürich which is industrial, progressive and increasingly secular in its dominant ethos, to mountain valleys in Catholic Switzerland, such as the Maderanertal, in which the middle ages still linger.

We are assured by St Paul that 'Evil communications corrupt good manners'. Maybe, but good communications corrupt them even more rapidly. Every improvement in communication, particularly in the dissemination of ideas, has an erosive effect on regional cultures. Compare, for instance, the statues and altars and stained glass prior to the period when the mass distribution of religious prints began, with the pictures and statues of Our Lord and the saints which date from the second half of the nineteenth century. The older artists were familiar with the work of their predecessors in their native valley or perhaps in some neighbouring town; they were not copyists. Even their least accomplished work was not wholly derivative. It had the rude vigour of genuine creative work. But in the nineteenth and still more in the twentieth century, the market was flooded by mass-produced religious pictures, prints and statues, with the deplorable results we all know.

### The factual element in the Haller-Rousseau idealization of the Bergler

Haller's idealization, which Rousseau adopted, of the Alpine peasant, uncorrupted by ambition and uninfected by avarice, was not wholly devoid of factual basis. It is, of course, absurd to maintain that the peasant is uninfected by avarice, but of all forms of avarice land hunger is the least ignoble, the land hunger so eloquently described by De Tocqueville.

The French peasant before the Revolution was, so De Tocqueville declares, '*si passionnément épris de la terre qu'il consacre à l'acheter toutes ses épargnes et l'achète à tout prix . . . il y enterre son coeur avec son grain. . . . Ce petit coin du sol qui lui appartient en propre dans ce vaste univers le remplit d'orgueil et d'indépendance.'*[1]

An important test of a healthy society is the proper distribution of power between town and country. Stalin's attempt to liquidate the Kulak would have been impossible had not all power in the State been transferred to the urban Marxists. In Switzerland the Bergler has still great influence politically, for the Swiss still agree, in the main, with the author of that mediaeval book, *A Christian Admonition*, who wrote: 'The farmer must in all things be protected and encouraged, for all depend on his labour, from the Emperor to the humblest of mankind, and his handiwork is particularly honourable and well-pleasing to God.'

Every great culture is born within the economy of the small town, village and farm.

*Fortunatus et ille deos qui novit agrestes.*

It was because Virgil 'knew the country gods' and because Wordsworth's 'daily teachers had been woods and hills' that Virgil and Wordsworth are of the company of immortals. It was no accident that the greatest poet of classical antiquity should have written the *Georgics* which is not only noble poetry but also a practical guide to farming.

Few would deny that an urban civilization is a greater danger to religion than life on the land. Jefferson, perhaps the greatest of the Founding Fathers of America, said that the proportion of other citizens to husbandmen in a State is the 'proportion of its unsound to its healthy parts. . . . I view great cities as pestilential to the morals, the health, and the liberties of man.'

Dr Alex Carrel, one of the world's greatest biologists and Nobel prizewinner, in his famous book, *Man the Unknown*, analyses the evil influence of an industrial civilization on mankind. He was particularly preoccupied with the flight from beauty. Here are some quotations from *Man the Unknown*:

'The descendants of the men who conceived and erected the monastery of Mont Saint-Michel no longer understand its splendour. They cheerfully accept the indescribable ugliness of the

---

[1] 'He is so passionately in love with the earth that he devotes all his savings to buying it, and buys it whatever the cost. He buries his heart with the seed. This little corner of the earth which belongs to him in all the vast universe fills him with pride and independence.' *L'Ancien Régime*, Liv. ii, Ch. i.

modern houses in Normandy and Brittany, and especially in the Paris suburbs.'

'During the history of a civilization, the sense of beauty, the moral sense, grows, reaches its optimum, declines and disappears.'

'Despite the marvels of scientific civilization, human personality tends to dissolve.'

'The peasant owning his land, the fisherman owning his boat, although obliged to work hard, are nevertheless masters of themselves and their time.'[1]

The Bergler is a democrat but he is a Tory democrat. He believes in progress but he does not despise tradition. He would agree with Burke that 'a people will not look forward to posterity who never looked back to their ancestors. A disposition to preserve and an ability to improve, taken together, would be my standard of a statesman.' Now Burke alone among his contemporaries diagnosed the true motive of the Jacobins, which was to transfer the balance of power from the country to the towns, and to use the country as a 'mere sustenance for the towns', a process completed in Soviet Russia but firmly checked in Switzerland where the interests of the peasants are still treated with great respect.

The Bergler in touch with nature is realistic in his political outlook, for Virgil's *justissima tellus* encourages no Utopian illusions. The 'most just earth' gives nothing for nothing. The peasant knows that man must sow before he can reap, and that a man must not only vote but also work for 'the more abundant life'.

There was, as I have tried to show in the preceding pages, some factual basis for Haller's idealization of the Bergler. Religion and the natural virtues have less to contend with in the mountains than in the cities. Even today divorce is not fashionable in mountain valleys, and marriages tend, in the main, to be stable. I know, of course, that the Bergler is in a state of transition, and that some of my observations are ceasing to be true of the modern Bergler. I remember feeling depressed by the evidence of change in the Lötschental. On the January day in 1909, when we climbed slowly from Kippel to the Lötschenlücke, the Lötschental was a lovely remote valley unconnected either by rail or motor road with the outer world. Today the railway

[1] *Man the Unknown*, pp. 130, 131, 293, 294.

station of Goppenstein on the Lötschberg line is at the entrance
to the Lötschental, and a motor road penetrates as far as Blatten.
In my youth there was not a house in the valley which one could
not look at but with pleasure, but today the valley is desecrated
by some very ugly modern buildings.

'You ask me,' a Swiss friend of mine said, 'whether the influence of the tourist on the Bergler has in the main been good.
Well, you know the Lötschental. A hundred years ago, life was
hard but the men and women who lived in this remote valley
were in the main happy. They had few wants. There was the
Church and the great Feast Days which gave colour to life and
still do, and the peasants would meet together and drink wine and
sing in chorus, but now they have become conscious of a larger
life with more pleasures and they are becoming dissatisfied. There
is now a plan to develop winter sports in the Lötschental, and
they will run up ski lifts and there will be cocktail bars and perhaps a winter sports variant of *La Dolce Vita*, and where will
it end?'

Yes, the winds of change are blowing through these mountain
valleys, bringing with them the seeds of scepticism in ultimate
values, the scepticism from which great civilizations have
perished in the past, for as Dr Monk Gibbon in his delightful
autobiography, *Mount Ida*, rightly says, 'The truth is that a
civilization collapses when the essential reverence for absolute
values which religion gives disappears. Rome discovered that in
the days of her decadence. Men live on the accumulated Faith
of the past as well as on its accumulated self-discipline. Overthrow these and nothing seems missing at first, a few sexual
taboos, a little of the prejudices of a Cato, these have gone by the
board. But something else has gone as well, the mortar which
held society together, the integrity of the individual soul; then
the rats come out of their holes and begin burrowing under the
foundations and there is nothing to withstand them.'

The rats are burrowing under the foundations of the Bergler
life, but though these foundations need to be reinforced, they
have not yet been irreparably undermined.

# INDEX

# Index

# Index

# Index

# Index

# GEORGE ALLEN & UNWIN LTD
London: 40 Museum Street, WC1

Auckland: 24 Wyndham Street
Bombay: 15 Graham Road, Ballard Estate, Bombay 1
Bridgetown: P.O. Box 222
Buenos Aires: Escritorio 454-459, Florida 165
Calcutta: 17 Chittaranjan Avenue, Calcutta 13
Cape Town: 109 Long Street
Hong Kong: 44 Mody Road
Ibadan: P.O. Box 62
Karachi: Karachi Chambers, McLeod Road
Madras: Mohan Mansions, 38c Mount Road, Madras 6
Mexico: Villalongin 32-10, Piso, Mexico 5, D.F.
Nairobi: P.O. Box 4536
New Delhi: 13-14 Asaf Ali Road, New Delhi 1
São Paulo: Avenida 9 de Julho, 1138-Ap. 51
Singapore: 36c Prinsep Street, Singapore 7
Sydney, N.S.W.: Bradbury House, 55 York Street
Tokyo: 10 Kanda-Ogawamachi, 3-Chome, Chiyoda-ku
Toronto: 91 Wellington Street West, Toronto 1